P9-DBI-645

THE
ROAD
TO
DAYBREAK

Books by Henri J. M. Nouwen

INTIMACY: Essays in Pastoral Psychology

CREATIVE MINISTRY

WITH OPEN HANDS

THE WOUNDED HEALER: Ministry in Contemporary Society

PRAY TO LIVE: Thomas Merton as a Contemplative Critic

AGING: The Fulfillment of Life

OUT OF SOLITUDE: Three Meditations on the Christian Life

REACHING OUT: Three Movements in the Spiritual Life

THE GENESEE DIARY: Report from a Trappist Monastery

THE LIVING REMINDER: Prayer and Service
in Memory of Jesus Christ

CLOWNING IN ROME: Reflections on Solitude, Celibacy,
Prayer and Contemplation

IN MEMORIAM

THE WAY OF THE HEART: Desert Spirituality and
Contemporary Ministry

CRY FOR MERCY: Prayers from the Genesee Monastery

MAKING ALL THINGS NEW: An Invitation to the Spiritual Life

COMPASSION: Reflections on the Christian Life

LETTER OF CONSOLATION

GRACIAS: A Latin American Journal

LOVE IN A FEARFUL LAND

LIFESIGNS: Intimacy, Fecundity, Ecstasy in Christian Perspective

BEHOLD THE BEAUTY OF THE LORD: Praying with Icons

Henri J. M. Nouwen

THE ROAD TO DAYBREAK

A Spiritual Journey

IMAGE BOOKS
DOUBLEDAY

NEW YORK LONDON TORONTO SYDNEY AUCKLAND

AN IMAGE BOOK
PUBLISHED BY DOUBLEDAY
a division of Bantam Doubleday Dell Publishing Group, Inc.
1540 Broadway, New York, New York 10036

IMAGE and DOUBLEDAY are trademarks of Doubleday,
a division of Bantam Doubleday Dell Publishing Group, Inc.

This book was originally published in hardcover
by Doubleday in 1988. First Image Books edition
published October 1990 by special arrangement with
Doubleday.

Library of Congress Cataloging-in-Publication Data
Nouwen, Henri J. M.
    The road to daybreak.
    1. Nouwen, Henry J. M.—Diaries.
2. Communauté de l'Arche.   I. Title.
BX4705.N87A3   1988   282'.092'4 [B]   88-3543
ISBN 0-385-41607-5

Acknowledgments

This journal could make it to publication only with the help of many friends. With much gratitude I mention their names.

During the time of writing, Peter Weiskel, who worked for me in Cambridge, Massachusetts, did the first editing on the handwritten text. Margaret Studier spent many hours typing, and Phil Zaeder gave much attention to the use of good English.

When I moved to Canada in August 1986 and decided to condense the long text into a readable book, Richard White offered his assistance in deciding which entries could form the core of a book and which could be deleted. He worked several months to discern the main direction of the seven-hundred-page manuscript by carefully evaluating the various entries.

During the last phase of the work, Michael Plante helped me to put the already condensed text into final form. During that period, Sue Mosteller and Michael Harank offered many suggestions for deletions, additions, and revisions. Connie Ellis, my secretary at Daybreak, was of invaluable help in retyping the whole text, asking permission of different people to publish entries in which their story was told and encouraging me to keep believing in the significance of this journal.

To all these friends I am deeply grateful. Their skillful assistance, their generosity in giving me their time and attention, and their personal interest made it possible to move from a seemingly unmanageable stack of papers to a text that could be presented to

Bob Heller, my editor at Doubleday. If ever a personal journal was the result of many people's work, it is *The Road to Daybreak*. I would like the reader of this book to know this and thus share in my gratitude.

Contents

THE
ROAD
TO
DAYBREAK

Prologue

In the late seventies, when I was on the faculty of Yale Divinity School, someone paid me a visit that would radically change my life. At the time it seemed like an uneventful and even inconsequential visit. But as the years went by I started to see it as a response to my prayer: "Lord, show me where you want me to go, and I will follow you."

And so it is that I begin this book with the story of this seemingly unimportant visit. One afternoon the bell of my New Haven apartment rang and a young woman stood at my door. She said, "I am Jan Risse and come to bring you greetings from Jean Vanier." I had heard about Jean Vanier and the L'Arche community for mentally handicapped people, but I had never met him, spoken to him, written him, or been in touch with his work. So I was quite surprised by these greetings and said, "Well, thank you . . . what can I do for you?" She said, "Oh . . . nothing. I just came to bring you the greetings of Jean Vanier." "Yes, I understand," I said, "but I guess you have another reason for your visit." But she insisted, "No, no. I just came to bring you greetings from Jean." It was hard for me to hear her. I kept thinking that her greetings were but the introduction to a request to give a lecture, a retreat, or a sermon or to write an article or a book. Convinced that her bringing greetings wasn't all she came for, I tried once more: "I appreciate hearing from Jean Vanier, but is there anything I can do for you?"

She smiled and said, "Well, can I come in?" I realized then that I hadn't shown much hospitality and said hastily, "Sure, sure, come in . . . but I have to leave soon because I have many appointments at the school." "Oh, you just go ahead," she replied, "and I will spend some quiet time here until you return."

When I returned that evening, I found my table set with a beautiful linen cloth, nice plates and silverware, flowers, a burning candle, and a bottle of wine. I asked, "What is this?" Jan laughed. "Oh, I thought I'd make you a nice meal." "But where did you find all these things?" I asked. She looked at me with a funny expression and said, "In your own kitchen and cupboards . . . you obviously don't use them too often!" It then dawned on me that something unique was happening. A stranger had walked into my home and, without asking me for anything, was showing me my own house.

Jan stayed for a few days and did many more things for me. Then, when she left, she said, "Just remember, Jean Vanier sends his greetings to you." A few years went by. I had completely forgotten about Jan's visit. Then one morning Jean Vanier called and said, "I am making a short silent retreat in Chicago. Would you like to join me?" Again, for a moment, I thought he wanted me to give a talk there. But he insisted. "Henri, it is a *silent* retreat. We can just be together and pray."

Thus Jean and I met. In silence. We spoke a bit, but very little. In the years that followed, I made two visits to his community in France. During my second visit I made a thirty-day retreat and gradually came to the realization that Jan Risse's visit had been the first of a series of events in which Jesus was responding to my prayer to follow him more fully.

But the years between Jan Risse's visit and my decision to become part of L'Arche were tumultuous and full of anxious searching. After ten years at Yale, I felt a deep desire to return to a more basic ministry. My trips to Latin America had set in motion the thought that I might be called to spend the rest of my life among the poor of Bolivia or Peru. So in 1981 I resigned from my teaching position at Yale and went to Bolivia to learn Spanish and to Peru to experience the life of a priest among the poor. My months there were so intense that I decided to keep a journal, which was later published under the title *Gracias!* I sincerely tried to discern whether living among the poor in Latin America was the direction to go. Slowly and painfully, I discovered that my spiritual ambitions were different from God's will for me. I had to face the fact that I wasn't capable of doing the work of a missioner in a Spanish-speaking country, that I needed more emotional support than my fellow missioners could offer, that the hard struggle for justice often left me discouraged and dispirited, and that the great variety of tasks and obligations took away my inner composure. It was hard to hear my friends say that I could do more for the South in the North than in the South and that my ability to speak and write was more useful among university students than among the poor. It became quite clear to me that idealism, good intentions, and a desire to serve the poor do not make up a vocation. One needs to be called and sent. The poor of Latin America had not called me; the Christian community had not sent me. My experience in Bolivia and Peru had been very fruitful, but its fruits were not the ones I had expected.

About that time Harvard Divinity School invited me to join their faculty to teach christian spirituality with a special emphasis on the spiritual aspects of liberation theology. I accepted with the conviction that I was called to a "reverse mission," a mission from the South to the North, and that in this way I could realize my desire to serve the church in Latin America. But I soon realized that the students had a greater need for spiritual formation than for information about the burning issues of the Latin American Church, and so my teaching quickly moved to more general areas of the spiritual life. Thus I found myself doing what I had done at Yale, only on a larger scale. Gradually I discovered that Harvard was not the place where I was called to follow Jesus in a more radical way; I was not really happy there, found myself somewhat sulky and complaining, and never felt fully accepted by the faculty or students. The signs were clear that I still had not found the way.

he midst of all my doubts and uncertainties, the voices of Jan

Risse, Jean Vanier, and L'Arche gained in strength. When I visited the L'Arche community in France I experienced a sense of at-homeness I had not experienced at Yale, in Latin America, or at Harvard. The noncompetitive life with mentally handicapped people, their gifts of welcoming me regardless of name or pres-tige, and the persistent invitation to "waste some time" with them opened in me a place that until then had remained unavailable to me, a place where I could hear the gentle invitation of Jesus to dwell with him. My sense of being called to L'Arche was based more on what I had to receive than on what I had to give. Jean Vanier said, "Maybe we can offer you a home here." That, more than anything else, was what my heart desired, even though I had never taken my desire seriously, and that gave me the first inkling that my prayer to follow Jesus more radically was being heard.

The core of this book consists of the spiritual journal I kept during the year between leaving Harvard and joining the L'Arche community of Daybreak in Canada. Most of that year I spent in Trosly-Breuil, where Jean Vanier first founded homes for people with mental handicaps. But I made many excursions to Holland, Germany, Canada, the United States, and other places. When I went to France, my hope was that L'Arche would prove to be the place where I would be called to follow Jesus. But I wasn't sure. In fact, the difference between the life of the university and the life at L'Arche proved to be so profound that I experienced many doubts about whether I would be able to make the jump. These journal notes show the struggle, yes, the spiritual combat con-nected with the question "How does one follow Jesus unreserv-edly?" Many of the same pains I expressed in *The Genesee Diary* and *Gracias!* can be found here. The difference is not only the context, but also the direction. In the past I wanted to know where to go. Now I knew where to go, but didn't really want to. Living and working with mentally handicapped people seemed precisely the opposite of what I had been trained and qualified to do. Every-thing else seemed more reasonable and useful than going to L'Arche. But still . . . Jan Risse, Jean Vanier, my friends at L'Arche, and most of all the handicapped people themselves kept saying, gently but persistently, "Here is a home for you; maybe you need us." All my desires to be useful, successful, and productive revolted. Some of my trips away from L'Arche may have been an expression of that revolt. But whether I knew it at the time or not, they became part of the basic struggle to let go of old ways and to be led to "where I rather would not go" (John 21:18).

In the following pages there are words about L'Arche, about prayer, about living with handicapped people, about art, about city life, about filmmaking, about AIDS, about the conflicts in the church, about Paris, London, San Francisco, and Los Angeles, about Canada and a future there, and about many other small and great people and events. What binds them together in their wide variety is the spiritual struggle to say "yes" to Jesus' invitation "Come and follow me." It is a screaming and kicking "yes" that fills these pages. It is a "yes" emerging from the recognition of my own brokenness and need for radical healing. In the epilogue I try to summarize my experiences during my first year at Daybreak, the L'Arche community in Toronto to which I went after my year in France. Even though I didn't have the time and energy to keep a journal at Daybreak, I still felt the need to describe simply and honestly what happened to me after I had found a home.

The title of this journal, *The Road to Daybreak*, not only refers to the fact that my year in Trosly led me to accept the invitation of the Daybreak community in Toronto. It also refers to my conviction that the experiences described in this journal led me to the beginning of a new life.

Many of these notes speak about confusion, fear, and loneliness, because much of the journey took place in the night. But as I stand at the break of a new day, I am filled with hope. I pray that those who will read this journal will be encouraged in their own spiritual journey and discover that same hope in their own hearts.

1

Parents and Children

A New Beginning

(Trosly, France; Tuesday, August 13, 1985)

This is the first day of my new life! Though it sounds melodramatic, I cannot avoid feeling that something significant is starting today. My decision to leave Harvard Divinity School and move to France to live for at least a year with Jean Vanier and his L'Arche community in Trosly took many tears and many sleepless nights. It came after a period of many hesitations and inner debates. But as I drove away from the carriage house which for a year had been the center of my life at Harvard, I felt as if I were moving toward a new freedom. When Madame Vanier, Jean's eighty-seven-year-old mother, threw her arms around me as I stepped into her house this morning, it felt like coming home.

It is so good to be back. Nine months ago I finished a thirty-day retreat here. At the time I had no idea I would be back so soon, but now I know that the retreat prepared me to say good-bye to the academic world and to start looking for a community of people who could lead me closer to the heart of God.

This afternoon I heard something like an inner voice telling me to start keeping a journal again. Ever since my trip to Latin America four years ago, I had given up daily writing. But it suddenly dawned on me that this year is going to be a year of prayer, reading, and writing while listening carefully to the inner movements of the spirit and struggling with the question "How do I follow Jesus all the way?" How better to keep in touch with God's work in me than by recording what is happening to me day after day? If this is really going to be a year of discernment, an honest journal might help me as much now as it has in the past.

The enormous contrast between my busy, noisy, and nerve-wracking last days in Cambridge and this utterly quiet, still day in Trosly moves me deeply. As I walked the narrow streets of this little French village this afternoon without seeing a person or hearing a car, I wondered if I were on the same planet. The six-and-a-half-hour night flight from Logan Airport in Boston to Charles de Gaulle Airport in Paris makes the distance between there and here seem so small. But Cambridge and Trosly are much farther apart than a night's flight. They represent two very different worlds: Cambridge—a world of academic intensity, institutional rivalry, intellectual competition, and ever mounting excitement; Trosly—a world of quiet village living, community celebration, the sharing of human vulnerabilities, and an always new invitation to let Jesus be the center of everything.

It is dark now, very dark. Not a sound around me, only the regular beat of the quartz alarm clock Jutta Ayer gave me shortly before I left. The clock reminds me of the world I left behind. Here no one has told me when to get up tomorrow, what to do, or whom to meet: no classes, interviews, or counseling, no last-minute phone calls or visits. Tomorrow is as open as any tomorrow has ever been. What will it bring? Only God knows. The silence whispers, "Go to bed and sleep as long as you want. Nobody will wake you up." I will push the button of my quartz clock to the white dot which reads "signal off." A new life has begun.

The Name Above All Other Names

(Wednesday, August 14)

The house in which I live is called "Les Marronniers." I had known the name, but only today did I find out its meaning. Madame Vanier told me that *les marronniers* are the four large chestnut trees standing in front of the house. "Each of them has a different name," she said, "Marc, Luc, Matthew, and Jean," and with a smile she added, "You will understand why I called the one closest to the house Jean."

Names are very important. For a long time I lived with the conviction that Francis Avenue, on which Harvard Divinity School stands, was named after St. Francis. That had somehow given me a little consolation as I walked to work. I must have suppressed my inclination to verify this conviction out of fear of being robbed of another illusion, but one day someone brought me back to earth by informing me that the Francis for whom the street was named was a nineteenth-century Divinity School professor and not my favorite saint. I am sure that no saints gave their names to any of Cambridge's streets or Harvard's houses. Here in Trosly the saints are everywhere and the community for the handicapped is called L'Arche, a constant reminder of Noah's Ark, to which people and animals fled for shelter as the flood covered more and more of the land. L'Arche is indeed the place where many vulnerable men and women who are threatened by the judgmental and violent world in which they live can find a safe place and feel at home.

Names tell stories, most of all the name which is above all other names, the name of Jesus. In his name I am called to live. His name has to become my house, my dwelling place, my refuge, my ark. His name has to start telling the story of being born, growing up, growing old, and dying—revealing a God who loved us so much that he sent his only child to us.

Père Thomas

(Thursday, August 15)

Today, August 15, the Feast of the Assumption of Our Lady, is a national holiday in France. Although the majority of French people seldom if ever enter a church, they all close their stores and businesses to celebrate this feast day of the Mother of God, to whom France is especially dedicated.

Père Thomas Philippe, a Dominican who twenty years ago started the L'Arche community with Jean Vanier and who is considered its spiritual father, offered a long, fervent homily in honor of Mary's assumption. The hundred and fifty people in the chapel all listened with great attention to the words of this eighty-year-old priest.

I keep hearing more and more about this saintly man. Father Ed O'Connor, who comes here every year from the United States to make a retreat with Père Thomas, calls him the John of the Cross of our time. This sounded rather grandiose at first, but when the Peeters, a Belgian family who invited me to dinner, told me that they had moved to France to be close to Père Thomas, I started to become aware of the extraordinary spiritual gifts of this man. I still have a hard time following his long and intense French sermons, but being in his presence and hearing the way he pronounces the words "Mary," "Our Mother," and "the Blessed Virgin," and speaks of the Assumption as a source of hope for all of us are experiences I cannot forget.

It is a profound experience to be in the presence of someone whom I can hardly understand, but who nevertheless communicates deeply and convincingly the mystery of God's presence among us. It is an especially profound experience since it unites me so intimately with the so-called "retarded" men and women and lets me hear as they do, with the heart. After the Eucharist,

Père Thomas shook my hand with great intensity and said, "I entrust my sheep to you, Father." I replied, "I will try my best, but with my French I can assure you my sermons will be a lot shorter!" He smiled.

This afternoon he left for ten days. One of the reasons I came just before his departure was to be able to take his place. One of the women said to me, "Père Thomas cannot be replaced, you know." Nevertheless, in the coming days I will try. Standing in for a saint will not be easy, but then again, God is merciful . . .

Danny's Prayer

(Friday, August 16)

Tonight I spent a wonderful evening with the L'Arche group from Cork, Ireland, who are spending the month of August in Trosly. It is obviously easier for me to be among the Irish than among the French. The language helps, but also the easy camaraderie.

During evening prayer we sang simple songs, we listened to Danny, one of the handicapped men from Cork, who with great difficulty read from Jean Vanier's book *I Meet Jesus,* and we prayed. Danny said, "I love you, Jesus. I do not reject you even when I get nervous once in a while . . . even when I get confused. I love you with my arms, my legs, my head, my heart; I love you and I do not reject you, Jesus. I know that you love me, that you love me so much. I love you too, Jesus." As he prayed I looked at his beautiful, gentle face and saw without any veil or cover his agony as well as his love. Who would not respond to a prayer like that?

I suddenly felt a deep desire to invite all my students from Harvard to sit with me there in that circle. I felt a deep love for all those men and women I had tried to speak to about Jesus and had often failed to touch. I wanted so much for all of them to sit and let Danny tell them about Jesus. I knew they would understand what

I had not been able to explain. As I walked home after having kissed everyone good-night, I felt a strange warm pain that had something to do with the many worlds I was trying to keep together.

L'Arche: A Little Bit of History

(Saturday, August 17)

Less than a minute's walk from the house where I live is the house where it all started. Above the door hangs a small wooden sign with the word "L'Arche." In that house Jean Vanier went to live twenty years ago with two handicapped men, Raphael and Philippe. Every time I pass that small, unspectacular little house and see the wooden sign above the door, I am moved by the mystery of small acts of faith. When Jean decided to take two handicapped men out of a large institution and bring them into his "ark," he knew he was doing something irreversible. He knew that from that moment on his life would be intimately connected with the lives of these two men. They had no family to which he could send them, nor could he ever return them to the institution from which they came. This was the form of poverty Jean had chosen after much prayer and a long search for a vocation.

When Jean made this decision he was still a professor of philosophy at St. Michael's College in Toronto. He had come to Trosly to visit his spiritual director, Père Thomas Philippe, who had been his guide and friend since the days of his studies at the Institut Catholique in Paris. Under the guidance and inspiration of Père Thomas, Jean was able to leave his successful academic career and embark on a spiritual journey, the end of which was completely invisible. As far as Jean was concerned, living with Raphael and Philippe was to be his vocation. He had no plans to start a large movement, nor was he thinking about an international network of homes for the handicapped. His new life began in this small

French village with a humble house and two handicapped men, and with his good friend Père Thomas nearby.

Today, L'Arche is a word that inspires thousands of people all over the world: in France, Belgium, Italy, Spain, Canada, the United States, Mexico, Haiti, Honduras, the Ivory Coast, India, and many other countries. Its vision is a source of hope; its work draws praise from popes, bishops, kings, queens, and presidents. But Jean didn't anticipate any of that when he put the L'Arche sign above the door of his first *foyer*. He just wanted to be poor with the poor.

It sounds very much like stories I have heard before—of Benedict and Scholastica, Francis and Claire, Peter Maurin and Dorothy Day, Catherine de Huyck Doherty and Frère Roger of Taize. "Set your heart on God's kingdom . . . these other things will be given you as well" (Luke 12:31).

Painful but Precious Memories

(Sunday, August 18)

A sunny Sunday! My father came to visit me. Traveling with a friend from Holland to Switzerland, he decided to come through Trosly to see where and how I am living now. He attended the Mass I celebrated for the L'Arche community, ate dinner with some of the members of La Ferme, the contemplative community founded by Père Thomas, visited the Irish group, and had tea with Madame Vanier.

It was a special joy to listen to the stories Madame Vanier and my father had to share. She was born in 1898, my father in 1903, and though their lives have followed quite different courses, they have common memories of a part of history I know only from books. Madame Vanier's experiences at the Canadian embassies in Paris, London, and Algiers and my father's experiences in a Dutch law firm and university were connected by their common experiences of the Second World War.

During the war years seven European governments were in exile in England. During that period the Vaniers lived in London as representatives of the Canadian government. They came to know, often in bomb shelters, Dutch officials who were quite well known to my father.

And here they were, drinking tea in 1985, talking about a time I scarcely remember. They mentioned names of people who were once quite famous but are now forgotten and relived frightening and exhilarating events which are hardly real for latecomers like me.

How strange that this cruel war was the context of my vocation to the priesthood and Jean Vanier's call to a life among the poor. Our parents taught us something about God that is hard to teach to a generation with no memories of bomb shelters, the destruction of large cities like Rotterdam and London, and the constant fear of death.

Seeing and hearing these two strong people speak with each other made me aware of a mystery of human and divine love far beyond words and gestures, revealed here for a moment in a casual encounter over tea.

2

Following Jesus

Leave Everything Behind and Follow Me

(Monday, August 19)

The story of the rich young man, which I read in both French and English during the Eucharist, continues to captivate me. "Jesus looked steadily at him and loved him, and he said, 'There is one thing you lack. Go and sell everything you own and give the money to the poor, and you will have treasures in heaven; then come, follow me.' But his face fell at these words and he went away sad, for he was a man of great wealth" (Mark 10:21–22).

Jesus loved this young man and, as I understand it, desired to have him with him as a disciple. But the young man's life was too complex; he had too many things to worry about, too many affairs to take care of, too many people to relate to. He couldn't let go of his concerns, and thus, disappointed and downcast, he left Jesus. Jesus was sad, the young man was sad, and today I feel sad because I wonder how different his life would have been had he been free enough to follow Jesus. He came, heard, but then left. We never hear of him again. Every year we remember Peter, John, and

James, the three disciples Jesus loved so much. But this man, whom Jesus also loved in a special way and also invited to become a witness to the good news, remains unknown. He never became a follower of Jesus and never made his mark on the history of the church as these other disciples did. If Francis of Assisi had remained in business, he would certainly not be remembered so fondly today.

I feel like praying tonight that my life might become simple enough for me to be able to say "yes" when Jesus looks at me with love and invites me to leave everything behind and follow him. Missing that moment would not only sadden Jesus and me but would, in a way, also be a refusal to take my true place in God's work of salvation.

Jessie's Threat

(Friday, August 23)

John Fraser, the European correspondent of the *Globe and Mail,* one of Canada's national newspapers, came to visit Madame Vanier. I was invited for tea. We talked about the people of China, Tibet and the Dalai Lama, the Catholic Church in the Philippines and North Korea, and the Pope's recent visit to Holland. John Fraser is a well-traveled, very knowledgeable journalist who is both a keen observer of world events and a man with a deep personal interest in the religious life.

Among all his stories about world events, John told us a small story about his daughter Jessie. It is this story I will remember most:

One morning when Jessie was four years old, she found a dead sparrow in front of the living room window. The little bird had killed itself by flying into the glass. When Jessie saw the dead bird she was both deeply disturbed and very intrigued. She asked her father, "Where is the bird now?" John said he didn't know. "Why did it die?" she asked again. "Well," John said hesitantly, "because all birds return to the earth." "Oh," said Jessie, "then we have to bury it." A box was found, the little bird was laid in the box, a paper napkin was added as a shroud, and a few minutes later a little procession was formed with Daddy, Mama, Jessie, and her little sister. Daddy carried the box, Jessie the homemade cross. After a grave was dug and the little sparrow was buried, John put a piece of moss over the grave and Jessie planted the cross upon it. Then John asked Jessie, "Do you want to say a prayer?" "Yes," replied Jessie firmly, and after having told her baby sister in no uncertain terms to fold her hands, she prayed: "Dear God, we have buried this little sparrow. Now you be good to her or I will kill you. Amen." As they walked home, John said to Jessie, "You didn't have to threaten God." Jessie answered, "I just wanted to be sure."

Well, among all the stories about the Pope, the Dalai Lama, and the other leaders of this world, Jessie's story told me most about the human heart: compassionate—but ready to kill when afraid. Whether we become merciful people or killers depends very much on who tells us what life is about. John, who had to tell so many stories about violence, murder, oppression, and other human sins, wanted Jessie to learn another story. His deep love for his family made that very clear.

Seeing and Being Seen

(Saturday, August 24)

Today we celebrate the feast of St. Bartholomew. I am struck by the first encounter between Jesus and Bartholomew, who in the Gospel is called Nathanael.

The emphasis is on *seeing*. Jesus said to Nathanael, "Before Philip came to call you, I saw you under the fig tree," and after Nathanael's response: "You are the Son of God," Jesus remarked, "You believe that just because I said I saw you under the fig tree.

You will see greater things than that . . . you will see heaven laid open, and above the Son of man, and the angels of God ascending and descending" (John 1:49–51).

The story speaks deeply to me since it raises the questions "Do I want to be seen by Jesus? Do I want to be known by him?" If I do, then a faith can grow which proclaims Jesus as the Son of God. Only such a faith can open my eyes and reveal an open heaven.

Thus, I will see when I am willing to be seen. I will receive new eyes that can see the mysteries of God's own life when I allow God to see me, all of me, even those parts that I myself do not want to see.

O Lord, see me and let me see.

God's Choice

(Sunday, August 25)

This morning Jean Vanier was interviewed on French television. I watched the program together with his mother, his brother Bernard, who is visiting for ten days, and Simone, a friend from the L'Arche house of prayer, La Ferme. Although I have heard Jean speak frequently, he said things that struck me as new.

A few minutes into the interview, Jean started to speak about Eric, a severely handicapped eighteen-year-old who had recently died. He mentioned Eric's deep sensitivity. Eric could not speak, walk, or feed himself, but when tension arose between assistants in the house, he banged his head against the wall; and when peace and harmony prevailed, he was joyful and cooperative. "The handicapped often tell us the truth, whether we want to know it or not," Jean remarked, and added with a smile, "It is not always easy to have such a barometer in your house."

As Jean mentioned this, I sensed that there is a deep connection between being seen by God and being seen by handicapped people. Yesterday's Gospel about Jesus seeing Nathanael suddenly held a new depth for me.

It was important for me to be reminded again of this gift of the handicapped. They see through a facade of smiles and friendly words and sense the resentful heart before we ourselves notice it. Often they are capable of unmasking our impatience, irritation, jealousy, and lack of interest and making us honest with ourselves. For them, what really counts is a true relationship, a real friendship, a faithful presence. Many mentally handicapped people experience themselves as a disappointment to their parents, a burden for their families, a nuisance to their friends. To believe that anyone really cares and really loves them is difficult. Their heart registers with extreme sensitivity what is real care and what is false, what is true affection and what is just empty words. Thus, they often reveal to us our own hypocrisies and invite us always to greater sincerity and purer love.

My limited experience with handicapped people has made me see the truth of Jean's observation. Being at L'Arche means many things, but one of them is a call to a greater purity of heart. Indeed, Jesus speaks through the broken hearts of the handicapped, who are considered marginal and useless. But God has chosen them to be the poor through whom he makes his presence known. This is hard to accept in a success- and production-oriented society.

God Is Not in a Hurry

(Monday, September 2)

When I was wondering what to write about tonight, I realized that I often write about my most immediate concerns, while the deeper stirrings of the spirit remain unrecorded.

Today I was reading *Two Dancers in the Desert,* a book by Charles Lepetit about the life of the spiritual father of the Little

Brothers and Sisters of Jesus, Charles de Foucauld. While reading it, I was reminded again of my deepest concern: how to come to a deeper experience of God in my life. I have been very concerned with this question since I feel that my life at Harvard led me in the wrong direction; that is why I finally left. Now that I am free to go the way of prayer, fasting, and solitude, I sense that without a concentrated effort I will transform my life here into another Harvard. I feel a burning desire to preach the Gospel, but I know in my heart that now is the time to pray, to read, to meditate, to be quiet, and to wait until God clearly calls me.

I am happy with the clarity I have. It makes no sense to preach the Gospel when I have allowed no time for my own conversion. This is clearly a time for hiddenness and withdrawal from lecturing and giving retreats, courses, seminars, and workshops. It is a time for being alone with God.

I feel a tension within me. I have only a limited number of years left for active ministry. Why not use them well? Yet one word spoken with a pure heart is worth thousands spoken in a state of spiritual turmoil. Time given to inner renewal is never wasted. God is not in a hurry.

Sheila Cassidy's Hospice

(Sunday, September 8)

Sheila Cassidy, the English doctor who was imprisoned and tortured two years after General Pinochet took power in Chile, has written me a fine letter. I have never met her, but our lives have occasionally touched each other's, mostly through our writings.

Today I read her short description of a hospice, and I was so touched by it that I would like to copy some of her words into this journal:

Medically speaking, hospices exist to provide a service of pain and symptom control for those for whom active anti-cancer treatment is no longer appropriate—there is *always* something that can be done for the dying, even if it's only having the patience and the courage to sit with them. Most lay people imagine that hospices are solemn, rather depress-ing places where voices are hushed and eyes downcast as patients and their families await the inevitable. Nothing could be further from the truth. Hospice care is about life and love and laughter, for it is founded upon two unshakable beliefs: that life is so precious that each minute should be lived to the full, and that death is quite simply a part of life, to be faced openly and greeted with the hand outstretched. One of the hallmarks of hospice life is celebration: cakes are baked and champagne uncorked at the first hint of a birthday or anniversary, and administrators, nurses, and volunteers clink glasses with patients and their families.*

As I read this, I was struck that much, if not all, that Sheila Cassidy says can be said of L'Arche as well. A hospice is for the dying who cannot be cured of their disease; L'Arche is for the handicapped whose handicap cannot be removed. Both proclaim loudly the preciousness of life and encourage us to face reality with open eyes and outstretched hands. Both are places of celebration in which the certainty of the present is always much more impor-tant than the uncertainty of the future. Both are witnesses to the paradox that the most unlikely people are chosen by God to make us see. Sheila Cassidy and Jean Vanier found their vocations in very different ways, but their common faith in Jesus and his Gospel has given them a remarkably similar vision.

* "Precious Spikenard," *Catholic New Times of Toronto,* 1985.

Leaving Harvard

(Monday, September 9)

My decision to leave Harvard was a difficult one. For many months I was not sure if I would be following or betraying my vocation by leaving. The outer voices kept saying, "You can do so much good here. People need you!" The inner voices kept saying, "What good is it to preach the Gospel to others while losing your own soul?" Finally, I realized that my increasing inner darkness, my feelings of being rejected by some of my students, colleagues, friends, and even God, my inordinate need for affirmation and affection, and my deep sense of not belonging were clear signs that I was not following the way of God's spirit. The fruits of the spirit are not sadness, loneliness, and separation, but joy, solitude, and community. After I decided to leave Harvard, I was surprised that it had taken me so long to come to that decision. As soon as I left, I felt so much inner freedom, so much joy and new energy, that I could look back on my former life as a prison in which I had locked myself.

I feel no regrets about my time at Harvard. Though in a divinity school, I had a real chance to be in a thoroughly secular university environment, and I had the opportunity to experience joy and fear in speaking directly about Jesus. I came to know many students and made some close friends, and saw more clearly than ever my own temptations and weaknesses. I feel warmly toward many of the people I met at Harvard, but now that I have left I also feel compassion for them. I now see so clearly that the ambition to achieve academically that keeps them bound is the same ambition that, without my fully knowing it, kept me bound too.

These thoughts came to me as I was reading one of St. Francis Xavier's letters from his mission field. In his youth he was a student and ambitious lecturer at the University of Paris. There he met

Ignatius of Loyola and became one of his first companions. He writes:

> Often I am overcome with the desire to cry out against the universities, especially against the University of Paris . . . and to rage with all my powers like a fool who has lost his senses.
>
> I would cry out against those who are more preoccupied with becoming scientists than with letting people in need profit from their science . . . I am afraid that many who learn their disciplines at the university are more interested in using them to acquire honors, bishoprics, privileges, and high position than in using them for what is just and necessary . . . The common word is: "I will study 'letters' in order to get some good privileged position in the Church, and after that I will live for God." These people are brutes, following the guidance of their sensuality and disordered impulses . . . They do not trust in God, nor do they give themselves completely to him . . . they are afraid that God does not want what they desire and that when they obey him they are forced to abandon their unjustly acquired privileges . . .
>
> How many would be enlightened by the faith of the Gospel if there were some who would put all their effort into finding good people who are willing to make sacrifices to search for and find not what belongs to them, but what belongs to Jesus Christ. In these lands so many people come to faith in Jesus Christ that many times my arms fail me because of the painful work of baptizing them.†

Francis Xavier wrote this many years after he had left the university. His new milieu, in which many people asked him to enlighten them with faith, made him see how many of those with whom he had lived and studied had been wasting their talents in the search for power and success and thereby were not available for the work of salvation that needed so urgently to be done.

---

† Xavier Léon-Dufour, *Saint François Xavier: Itinéraire Mystique de l'Apôtre*, La Colombe, Edition du Vieux Colombier, Paris, 1953, pp. 34–35.

Little has changed since the sixteenth century. After only a few weeks away from the competitive, ambitious, career-oriented life at Harvard Divinity School, I already feel the desire to say some of the things that Francis Xavier said. But it seems better not to play the prophet. I am not a Francis Xavier, nor do I wish to be. My dominant feeling toward Harvard is not indignation, but gratitude. Notwithstanding its pretentiousness, Harvard was the place where I met some of my most caring friends, where I became most acutely aware of my desire to love Jesus without compromise, and where I discovered my vocation to live and work with mentally handicapped people. Without a Harvard there probably would not have been a L'Arche for me either.

3

Darkness and Light

Feeling Rejected

(September 10)

A very hard day. I have been waiting for my dear friend Jonas, who took me to the airport in Boston and promised to come and visit me in France. Two weeks ago I heard he had indeed left for Paris and was going to visit me at the end of last week. Today I found out that he has already returned to Boston.

It was a very painful discovery. I had anticipated his visit and made all sorts of arrangements to welcome him. Now I feel not only sad at not seeing him, but also hurt and rejected. He did not even send me a note or a card and left me guessing and misguessing for a week.

I had had the impression that he was eager to see me and that one of the reasons he came to France was to be with me. He went to Brussels, Paris, and the Alps, but didn't come to Trosly! What a lesson! When I called him, he explained to me that things had just worked out differently from what he had foreseen, that he couldn't find my phone number, and that he was very tired. Still, I felt deeply hurt.

I now wonder what to do with this experience. Luckily, I am less depressed by it than I used to be in similar circumstances. Ever since I heard that Jonas had returned to Boston, I have been saying to myself, "If you really want to be less visible, less known, try to take this event and use it to become more forgotten, more passed over; be grateful for the occasion. Trust that hiddenness will give you new eyes to see yourself, your world, and your God. People cannot give you new eyes; only the one who loves you without limits."

I said things like this at different times, but it didn't quite work. I prayed for a few quiet moments, asking Jesus to help me not to become angry or bitter, and I tried to do my work as best I could. But I kept going back over the event again and again, constructing reasons for why he should have visited me and why I should feel rejected. It will probably take a while before I can fully forgive Jonas and be grateful for this occasion to grow in the spirit. Meanwhile, I am trying to keep a sense of humor and write a few notes to people who are always close to thinking that I am rejecting them.

Lord, give me the peace and joy that only you can give.

Icons and Iconography

(Sunday, September 15)

This afternoon I spent a few hours with Brother Christian Leisy, a monk of Christ in the Desert Monastery at Abiquiu, New Mexico, and Jackie Nelson from Santa Fe. They are both iconographers who have just finished a course with Father Egon Sendler, S.J., the great icon specialist. This occasion gave me a wonderful chance to ask questions about icon making which I had always wanted to ask.

I felt awe for these two humble and receptive people, who told me everything I wanted to know. What impressed me most was their conviction that the renewal of the art of iconography was in fact a renewal of the spiritual life. Not only did Brother Christian and Jackie Nelson exercise their art as a sacred task for which they had to be spiritually prepared, they also saw their work as a way to bring people to faith in the presence of the divine among us. They told me about many people who had found God through their interest in icons.

Icons are not just pious pictures to decorate churches and houses. They are images of Christ and the saints which bring us into contact with the sacred, windows that give us a glimpse of the transcendent. They need to be approached in veneration and with prayer. Only then will they reveal to us the mystery they represent.

Iconography has come to the West mainly from the Orthodox tradition, especially from Russia and Greece. Since the Russian Revolution of 1917, many Orthodox Christians have fled to the West, and through them the holy art of iconography has gradually become more known and appreciated in the Latin Church. Russian and Greek icons have become one of the most important sources of inspiration for my own prayer life. The icon of Our Lady of Vladimir, Rublev's icon of the Holy Trinity, and the nineteenth-century Greek icon of Christ that I obtained in Jerusalem have become integral parts of my life of prayer. I cannot think about the Holy Trinity, Jesus, and Mary without seeing them as the holy iconographers saw them. Icons are certainly one of the most beautiful gifts of the Orthodox Church to the churches of the West.

Brother Christian showed me photographs of the icons he had made and explained to me how he made them. He told me how he prepared the wood, how he mixed egg white with ground colors and made egg tempura, how he covered the surface with many layers of paint, going from the darker colors to the lighter, and how he did all of this in a way faithful to centuries-old iconographic traditions.

I was most moved by the icon of the Lebanese St. Charbel, whose face was one of the most penetrating I had ever seen on an icon. I asked Brother Christian if there were any chance that he could paint an icon of St. Charbel for me. He showed great interest in doing so. He is going to Rome for three years to study theology

and prepare himself for the priesthood. He hopes to set up his own
icon studio there. If he does, he will paint another Charbel icon for
me. It would be a wonderful way for me to stay in communion
with this remarkable Lebanese saint and his war-torn country.

A Sacred Connection

(Tuesday, September 17)

Two places in Trosly have a deep connection with each other.
They are L'Oratoire and La Forestière. L'Oratoire is a prayer
room where the Blessed Sacrament is exposed all day long and
where people are always present in silent adoration. The room
itself is a large, rather dark space with small kneelers and little
mats. The space is divided by a thick stone wall built of heavy grey
stone. In the middle of the wall, a large open space is carved in the
shape of a semicircle. There the monstrance stands, flanked on
each side by three oil lamps. Beautiful fresh flowers are always
present. On both sides of the wall people kneel, sit, or lie down in
prayer.

In many ways L'Oratoire is the heart of L'Arche. The unceasing silent prayer in the presence of the hidden God who gives
himself completely to us in unlimited love is the breath that makes
L'Arche possible. Every time I enter L'Oratoire I feel a deep rest
coming over me, and even if it is hard for me to pray I feel held
there. It is as if the room prays for me. I know of few places where
the presence of prayer is so tangible. If I can't pray, I go there so
that I can at least breathe air rich with prayer. In L'Oratoire I
meet the poverty of God, the God who became flesh and even our
food and drink, the God who does not hold back any of his love and
who says, "Eat of me, drink of me," the God who is so deeply
hidden that he can be recognized only by the eye of faith.

Then there is La Forestière, the foyer where the most handicapped people live with their assistants. The handicapped people

in La Forestière cannot walk, speak, or dress themselves. Many cannot feed themselves; some can hardly see or hear. Their bodies are severely distorted and often wracked with intense pain. When I go to La Forestière, I am always struck by the silence. The handicapped and their assistants live a life that in many ways feels monastic. The assistants are very busy with cleaning, cooking, feeding, dressing, or just holding, but they do it all in a very quiet way. Once in a while the quiet is interrupted by a groan, a cry, or a shout, in which the deep agony of the handicapped men and women can be sensed. But mostly there is silence.

If I can truly believe that God loved us so much that he became flesh among us, the people at La Forestière invite me to see how deep that love is. Indeed, here I can meet Jesus, the same Jesus whom I adore in L'Oratoire. Here, too, God is hidden; here, too, is unceasing prayer of simple presence; here, too, is the utmost poverty.

Tony, an Englishman who is also in Trosly for a year, said to me yesterday, "The first great commandment is lived out in L'Oratoire, the second in La Forestière. Here in Trosly you can come to understand what Jesus meant when he said that these commandments resemble each other." I have thought about Tony's words the whole day.

"Useless" Prayer

(Wednesday, September 18)

Why should I spend an hour in prayer when I do nothing during that time but think about people I am angry with, people who are angry with me, books I should read and books I should write, and thousands of other silly things that happen to grab my mind for a moment?

The answer is: because God is greater than my mind and my

heart, and what is really happening in the house of prayer is not measurable in terms of human success and failure.

What I must do first of all is be faithful. If I believe that the first commandment is to love God with my whole heart, mind, and soul, then I should at least be able to spend one hour a day with nobody else but God. The question as to whether it is helpful, useful, practical, or fruitful is completely irrelevant, since the only reason to love is love itself. Everything else is secondary.

The remarkable thing, however, is that sitting in the presence of God for one hour each morning—day after day, week after week, month after month—in total confusion and with myriad distractions radically changes my life. God, who loves me so much that he sent his only son not to condemn me but to save me, does not leave me waiting in the dark too long. I might think that each hour is useless, but after thirty or sixty or ninety such useless hours, I gradually realize that I was not as alone as I thought; a very small, gentle voice has been speaking to me far beyond my noisy place.

So: Be confident and trust in the Lord.

Joy in Small Corners

(Thursday, September 19)

Nathan, a Canadian assistant, invited me tonight for supper at his foyer, Le Surgeon. *Le surgeon* means "the shoot." It is also the French word for "the branches of the vine."

Le Surgeon in Cuise, a neighboring village, is a foyer for severely handicapped people like those at La Forestière. There I met Philippe, Sylvienne, Michelle, Jean-Luc, and Gérard, all people who need total care. Alain was temporarily in the hospital. Nathan told me a little about the daily schedule, much like a monastic schedule, in which every hour is carefully planned.

The days have a strict rhythm: dressing, bathing, eating breakfast, cleaning the house, shopping, cooking and eating dinner, quiet time, Mass, supper, getting ready for bed, and evening prayer. During the morning and afternoon the handicapped men and women spend a few hours in the "workshop," where other helpers do exercises with them to keep them as alert as possible. During these hours the assistants do housework and shopping and have their quiet time. During the night, one of the assistants sleeps close to their six handicapped companions to help them if needed. All the handicapped need different types of medication to maintain their physical and mental balance. The assistants hold frequent meetings with a psychiatrist and psychologist to discuss various complications in this small community.

Living in Le Surgeon requires great discipline and much commitment. It is a humble life in which joy is hidden in small corners, always there to be found but never separate from much pain. The atmosphere in Le Surgeon is peaceful and quiet with no great events or great debates, just simple, steady service, day in and day out. The rewards are small but very real: Philippe smiles, Jean-Luc looks you in the eye, Gérard gives a hug, Michelle sleeps a whole night, Sylvienne says one more word.

Nathan shows me pictures: "Look, this is Gérard when he came out of the institution, and here he is a year later. See the difference? Isn't that wonderful? Look how happy he is!" Indeed, Gérard is happy. He cannot walk, speak, dress, or undress himself, but with his smile he gives you all you could ever want.

During evening prayer one of the assistants reads a passage from Jean Vanier's book *I Walk with Jesus:* "There is an intimate connection between the presence of Jesus in the Eucharist and the presence of Jesus in the deprived person. The deprived person sends us back to Jesus in the Eucharist. To receive the Body of Jesus is to have his eyes and his heart to see him in the poor."

As Nathan drove me home, he said, "Dominique, one of the assistants at Le Surgeon, has decided to enter a contemplative monastery, and another of us is considering doing the same."

After my visit, I could well understand why.

The Pilgrims of Emmaus

(Saturday, September 21)

Today I went to the Louvre in Paris with Brad Wolcott to see Rembrandt's *The Pilgrims of Emmaus.* Brad and I met for the first time many years ago, when I was teaching at Yale Divinity School and he was finishing his dissertation in French literature. We became friends and lived through many struggles together. After a few years of teaching at St. Lawrence University in upstate New York, Brad decided to come to L'Arche and live here as an assistant in one of the foyers. It is a great joy for me to be so close to Brad again. Seeing *The Pilgrims of Emmaus* together has been our longtime hope.

At first sight, the painting was a disappointment. It was much smaller than I had expected and surrounded by so many other paintings that it was hard to see it as a separate work of art. Maybe I was too familiar with it through reproductions to be genuinely surprised. Brad and I stood in front of it just looking at the event portrayed.

Jesus sits behind the table looking up in prayer while holding a loaf of bread in his hands. On his right, one of the pilgrims leans backwards with his hands folded; while on his left, the other has moved his chair away from the table and gazes with utter attention at Jesus. Behind him a humble servant, obviously unaware of what is happening, reaches forward to put a plate of food on the table. On the table, a bright white cloth only partially covers the heavy table rug. There are very few objects on the table: three pewter plates, a knife, and two small cups. Jesus sits in front of a majestic stone apse flanked by two big, square pillars. On the right side of the painting, the entrance door is visible, and there is a coat stand in the corner over which a cape has been casually thrown. In the left corner of the room, a doglike figure can be seen lying under a bench. The whole painting is in endless varieties of brown: light brown, dark brown, yellow-brown, red-brown, and so on. The source of light is not revealed, but the white tablecloth is the brightest part of the painting.

Brad and I noticed that the bare feet of Jesus and the two pilgrims were painted with great detail. Not so the feet of the servant. Rembrandt obviously wanted us to know about the long, tiring walk they had just made. The large door and the cape on the coat stand were also there to remind us of the journey. These men truly came from somewhere.

As we looked at the painting, many people passed by. One of the guides said, "Look at Jesus' face, in ecstasy, yet so humble." That expressed beautifully what we saw. Jesus' face is full of light, a light which radiates from his head in a cloudlike halo. He does not look at the men around him. His eyes look upward in an expression of intimate communion with the Father. While Jesus is in deep prayer, he yet remains present; he remains the humble servant who came to be among us and show us the way to God.

The longer we looked at the painting, the more we felt drawn into the mystery it expresses. We gradually came to realize that the unoccupied side of the table across from Jesus is the place for the viewers. Brad said, "Now I see that Rembrandt painted the Eucharist, a sacramental event to which we, as we view it, are invited." It suddenly dawned on me how many similarities exist between this painting and Rublev's Trinity icon. There, as here, the white table is the real center. There, as here, the viewer is made a real part of the mystery of the Eucharist. As we continued to let the painting speak to us, we were amazed that we both came to see it more and more as a call to worship Christ in the Eucharist. The hands of Jesus holding the bread on the white altar table are the center not only of the light, but also of the sacramental action. Yet if Jesus were to leave the altar, the bread would still be there. And we would still be able to be with him.

For an instant the museum became a church, the painting a sanctuary, and Rembrandt a priest. All of it told me something about God's hidden presence in the world.

When we walked away from the painting and merged with

the crowd of tourists headed for the *Mona Lisa* and the *Venus de Milo*, we felt as if we were returning to a busy street after a time of silent adoration in a holy place.

Shifting Emotions

(Monday, September 23)

The depression that hit me when my long-awaited friend Jonas did not come to visit never totally left me. The many things to see, to hear, and to do covered up my darker feelings most of the time, but on various occasions they reappeared above the surface of my daily activities and reminded me of their presence.

This afternoon Jonas suddenly telephoned from the United States. My depression returned to me in full force. "Why didn't you call me? Why didn't you write me? Why didn't you visit me?" He responded, "Hey, wait a moment, that's all past. I want to come visit you in October!" I had a hard time hearing him. I kept nurturing my own hurt feelings and couldn't really appreciate his attempt to let me know that he really wanted to be a caring, loving friend who had not forgotten me.

Only after we discussed dates and places did I start to realize my deafness and gradually hear his faithful friendship. When I laid down the receiver, I felt new peace entering into my innermost self and sensed that my depression was slowly dissolving.

Oh, I am so little in control of my feelings and emotions! Often I have to just let them pass through me and trust that they won't hang around too long. Many other things happened today that could fill pages of this journal, but the few minutes with Jonas on the telephone affected me more than anything else. That is why I want to write about it, although it seems such a miserable subject after *The Pilgrims of Emmaus*. But often the deepest pains are hidden in the smallest corners.

4

First Glimpses of a
New Vocation

A New Community

(Toronto, Canada; Tuesday, October 1)

I am in Canada for nine days to visit Daybreak, the L'Arche community near Toronto. This is my first day. Joe Egan, the director, welcomed me warmly.

This morning I had a chance to meet all the assistants in their weekly meeting, and tonight I celebrated the Eucharist for all those who have been part of the community longer than two years, the handicapped as well as the assistants. It was interesting to hear Joe say that the distinction between handicapped people and assistants is becoming less important than the distinction between long-term community members and short-term helpers. Joe said that those who have built a real and lasting bond with L'Arche are especially responsible for making visitors, short-term assistants, and new handicapped people feel welcome.

So, indeed, it is a community on a journey, always changing, always adapting itself to new people, always open to surprises, always willing to try new things, but with a solid center of committed people who know the importance of permanency.

Meeting Michael

(Wednesday, October 2)

The Daybreak community is much larger than I had imagined. At the farm, about a thirty-minute drive from downtown Toronto, there are three homes for handicapped people and their assistants. The same land holds the homes of the assistant director, the farm manager, and their families. There is also a large, newly built meeting house, a carpenter's shop, and a large barn. The Daybreak community also includes three homes in the town of Richmond Hill and two in Toronto. The whole community—handicapped people, assistants, and staff—adds up to about eighty persons.

I am living at the "Green House" on the farm, a spacious house for six handicapped people and their assistants. It feels very good to be part of their daily life. Although all the handicapped people do some form of work during the day, they can never be left alone. This became dramatically clear with Michael, a very beautiful young man who suffers from frequent epileptic seizures. Even though he has regular medical care and takes all the necessary medication, he is often overcome by spasmodic attacks that can cause him serious injury. Tonight at the swimming pool in town, when he was left for a minute, he had a seizure, fell and hit his head on the concrete floor, and had to be taken to the hospital. Happily enough, his wound was not very serious and he could come home again soon.

In his slow, stuttering voice, he asked me to pray for him. After we had prayed for a while together, he gave me a big hug and a wonderful smile. Then he told me that he would like to help me say Mass and wear a red stole as I do. Michael may well be much closer to God than I am, and I will surely give him something to wear that makes him aware of how special he is.

Praying for Rose

(Thursday, October 3)

After dinner tonight a few of the community went to the chapel to pray for Rose. Rose is a twenty-two-year-old woman but looks like a fourteen-year-old girl, very thin, fragile, very wounded, but exceedingly beautiful. She cannot speak and can hardly walk, but she is a source of joy for all those who are close to her, especially for Mary, who assists her during the day.

Rose has suddenly become very ill and will soon need an operation. So we gathered around a candle and a red rose. Mary showed us some lovely slides of Rose, and then we all prayed for her. When handicapped people pray for handicapped people, God comes very near. The simplicity, directness, and intimacy of their prayer often make me feel like a skeptical bystander. I even feel a certain jealousy of their special gift of prayer. But they do not want me to be jealous. They hugged and kissed me after the prayer, and Michael took me by the hand to the sacristy to show me the red stole he wants to wear.

Lord, give me a heart like these people have so that I may understand more fully the depth of your love.

Slow Together Is Better
Than Fast Alone!

(Friday, October 4)

During the meeting of the long-term assistants, Nick, who works with four handicapped men in the wood shop, spoke about his joys and frustrations. He explained how hard it is to do a job well and at the same time keep the needs of the handicapped men uppermost in mind. He wants to become a skillful and efficient carpenter, but realizes that the products of his work are less important than the growing self-esteem of the men he works with. This requires a lot of patience and a willingness to let others do slowly what you yourself can do rapidly. It means always choosing work in which people much less capable than yourself can participate. It asks for a deep inner conviction that a slow job done together is better than a fast job done alone.

Nick told us how long it had taken him to come to this insight. At first he had been primarily concerned about learning the skills of carpentry from Joe, the director of the wood shop. He was very excited about learning a new trade. But then he came to see that his skills were meant not just to make blackboards, play blocks, and coat hangers for kindergartens, but also and above all to help four handicapped people grow in human dignity and self-reliance.

I found this out myself this afternoon when I went apple picking with Janice, Carol, Adam, Rose, and their assistants. My attitude was to get the apples picked, put them in bags, and go home. But I soon learned that all of that was much less important than to help Rose pick one or two apples, to walk with Janice looking for apples that hang low enough so that she herself can reach them, to compliment Carol on her ability to find good apples, and just to sit beside Adam in his wheelchair under an apple tree and give him a sense of belonging to the group.

We finally collected four bags of apples, but eight people took more than an hour to do it. I could have done the work in half an hour. But efficiency is not L'Arche's most important word. Care is.

Gregory's Story

(Saturday, October 5)

Today I visited the two L'Arche houses in the city, the house on Wolverleigh Boulevard and the house on Avoca Avenue.

At the Wolverleigh house, Gregory, one of the handicapped men in the house, gave a slide show about his own life. It was a very moving experience to hear a thirty-year-old man speak about the difference between his life in an institution and his life in a community. For Gregory, it was the difference between darkness and light, hell and heaven, self-destructive thoughts and a desire to live, between the "dumps" and a home.

When he was four years old, Gregory was taken to a mental institution in Orillia. "I had a stroke that paralyzed my right arm, and my parents brought me to Orillia. They came to see me every three weeks, but I was always sad because I didn't know why they put me there." Gregory showed slides of the dormitory, the dining hall, and the clothes room of the place where he had lived for twenty years, together with hundreds of other mentally handicapped people. He said, "We didn't have any privacy. We didn't even have our own clothes. We always wore clothes that had been worn before by other inmates. It was so lonely, so sad, I often thought of killing myself."

Then he showed slides of his life at Wolverleigh, to which he had come five years before. "Here I am in a store, buying food for the first time. And here I am in the kitchen, cooking my first meal. I was quite nervous, but everyone said they liked it."

Then he showed a slide of all the members of the house, sitting around the table with a candle in the middle. Gregory said, "Here we are all together at evening prayer. We never did such a thing in the institution. Here we are a family."

Gregory's simple but penetrating presentation taught me

more about the charism of L'Arche than any article I had read or lecture I had heard. L'Arche offers a home to broken people and gives them a new sense of dignity and self-respect. Gregory made the point and made it stick.

Raymond's Accident

(Sunday, October 6)

Everyone's mind and heart is with Raymond, who has been hit by a car and seriously injured.

Yesterday afternoon he and Bill were going to take a bus into town when Raymond suddenly crossed busy Yonge Street to reach the bus stop. Bill realized that Raymond had not noticed a car coming and tried to call him back. But Raymond did not hear him and was hit by the car and thrown into the air. At first it seemed that he had only minor fractures. But the X rays showed that many ribs were broken and one of his lungs was perforated. He is now in critical condition at St. Michael's Hospital in Toronto.

The whole community is visibly in anguish over it, especially D.J., the head of the house where Raymond lives, and Bill, who saw it all happen in front of his eyes. I became more acutely aware of the awesome responsibility assumed by people who care for handicapped men and women. On the one hand, you want to protect them as much as possible; on the other hand, you want to give them their independence as much as possible. It is a fine line to walk between these two "wants."

D.J. is a very responsible, caring person. He had felt that Bill and Raymond could travel together without assistance. They had done so for a long time. Now he obviously wonders if he gave them too much independence.

I went twice to St. Michael's Hospital with Kathy Judge to visit Raymond. Although on a respirator and fed intravenously, he was able to respond to our questions with nods. We prayed with him and assured him of our love. It was so sad to see him unable to talk to us. A few times he tried to pull off the respirator to say a few words but had to be restrained from doing so.

If he survives the first forty-eight hours, his chances for recovery are good. But his situation is quite critical. During the Eucharist this morning and the evening prayers in the different homes, all the prayers were for Raymond. These direct, heartfelt, and intense prayers revealed the strong faith of these handicapped people and their assistants. I felt surrounded by a fellowship of the weak. The noisy road in front of the house suddenly sounded like a "roaring lion, looking for someone to devour" (1 Peter 5:8).

O Lord, remember Raymond and give him your light and your joy during these agonizing hours. Please be good to him and all the broken people at Daybreak.

The Agony of Parents

(Monday, October 7)

Many things today. An intimate, prayerful liturgy with the assistants, an insightful presentation by Joe Vorstermans, the director of the wood shop, about work with handicapped people, a stimulating exchange among the new assistants about their experiences at Daybreak during the past week, and a lovely dinner and good conversation with Gus, the assistant director, his wife, and his children.

But the overriding concern was Raymond. His situation has deteriorated, and his death seems imminent. At 7:30 P.M. Gus, D.J., and I drove to Toronto, where Joe Egan, the director of Daybreak, joined us. When we got to the hospital we found Raymond so heavily sedated that he could not communicate with us any more. The doctor and nurse said there was still hope but also prepared us for a sudden turn for the worse. Most important of all was our time with Ray's parents.

It is hard for parents to see any child suffer. But to see the suffering of a handicapped child creates an even greater pain. Raymond had lived for years in an institution and had only recently come to Daybreak. Not everyone was convinced yet that Daybreak was the best place for Raymond, and the accident obviously called up feelings not only of guilt, but also of frustration and even anger. Many questions went through our minds concerning road safety, the freedom given to handicapped people, care for Ray, and the wisdom of past decisions.

Guilt feelings separate, divide, alienate; they can lead to anger and hostility. When we all came together in our common concern for Raymond, we were able to express our feelings to each other not only in words, but also in gestures of love and in prayers and stories about our lives. Soon a new community developed. Raymond's father said to Gus and D.J., "You are as much fathers to Raymond as I am," and thus acknowledged our pain. We were able to understand why he had not always been grateful for the work Daybreak had done for his son, and thus acknowledged his deep anguish.

Raymond's situation remains critical. We do not even know if he will survive the night. But all those who love him are united and support each other in their struggle. Not guilt but love guides our concern. And that certainly is a tangible way in which God has responded to our prayers.

A New Future Dawns

(Wednesday, October 9)

I am writing in a plane somewhere between Toronto and Paris. This morning I still wasn't sure if I should return to Trosly today. Raymond's condition remained critical. Last night Joe Egan said, "It might be good if you stay a few more days. In case Raymond does not survive this crisis, your presence will be very important for all of us." I promised to stay if the community asked me to.

But around 10 A.M. Ray's father called and told us good news: Ray was doing a little better. There was no immediate danger of death. Everyone agreed that I should return to Trosly as planned. At 1 P.M. I went with Kathy and D.J. to the hospital to say good-bye to Raymond and his parents. Raymond was still in the intensive care unit but indeed seemed a little better. He responded with nodding and hand squeezing to our questions, and his fever was clearly less than yesterday. I showed Ray's father how to make the sign of the cross on Ray's forehead. He had never done this before and cried as he signed his son in the name of the Father, the Son, and the Holy Spirit. A father's blessing is so healing.

Kathy, D.J., Ray's parents, and I sat together in the waiting room for a while and talked. We talked about Ray, about guilt and forgiveness, about trips to Paris, about how good it was to have each other's support, about crying and laughing, and about staying in touch and seeing each other again. After we left the hospital, Kathy and D.J. drove me to the airport; at 6:30 P.M. Air France flight 832 was on its way to Paris.

In my nine days at Daybreak I came to feel intimately a part of the intense joys and sorrows of this community of care. I have a deep love for the handicapped men and women and their assistants, who all received me with such warm hospitality. They did not hide anything from me. They allowed me to see their fears and their love. I feel deeply grateful for having been part of it all. I know that these days will deeply affect not only my time in France but also my decisions about the years to come.

5

The Primacy of the Heart

Writing Letters

(Trosly; Friday, October 11)

It feels good to be home again, even though the mail seems a little overwhelming. But as I was writing letters today, I realized that writing letters is a much more intimate way of communicating than making phone calls. It may sound strange, but I often feel closer to friends I write to than to friends I speak with by phone.

When I write I think deeply about my friends, I pray for them, I tell them my emotions and feelings. I reflect on our relationship, and I dwell with them in a very personal way. Over the past few months I have come to enjoy letter writing more and more. In the beginning it seemed like a heavy burden, but now it is a relaxing time of the day. It feels like interrupting work for a conversation with a friend.

The beauty of letter writing is that it deepens friendships and makes them more real. I have also discovered that letter writing makes me pray more concretely for my friends. Early in the morning, I spend a little time praying for each person to whom I have written and promised my prayers.

Today I feel surrounded by the friends I am writing to and praying for. Our love for each other is very concrete and life-giving. Thank God for letters, for those who send them, and for those who receive them.

Staying Home Can Be Following, Too!

(Sunday, October 13)

When Anthony heard Jesus' words to the rich young man, "Go and sell everything you own and give the money to the poor, then come, follow me" (Mark 10:21), he suddenly realized they were meant for him. He sold everything, left his family, and went into the desert. We now consider him the father of Christian monasticism. Today Madame Vanier told me how the same words that had led Anthony to the desert had brought her to L'Arche. After her husband died, she was living in an apartment in Montreal. When she came to visit her son in Trosly, one of the assistants said to her, "Why don't you come to live and work with us?" She answered brusquely, "Mind your own business, young man." But a seed was planted. When she made a retreat later that year to discern her future, she read this Gospel and suddenly felt tears welling up in her. She knew she had to follow the suggestion of the "brash" young man. She left her aristocratic life behind and came to live with her son in the community of L'Arche.

But today the story of the rich young man has a different meaning for her. Her poor health prevents her from traveling. It was her custom to return to Canada each year to visit her sons, Benedict and Michel, but for the first time in fourteen years at L'Arche she was unable to go. Her daughter, Thérèse, had come from England to visit before going to Canada. Madame Vanier's original plan had been to go with Thérèse, but now Thérèse was going alone.

As we read the Gospel story, it became clear that staying home now at eighty-seven had become as hard for her as leaving home at seventy-three. Now, leaving father, mother, brother, and sister to follow Jesus meant accepting the hard fact of no longer being able to visit her children in her own country and realizing that it might never be possible again.

It struck me that selling what you own, leaving your family and friends, and following Jesus is not a once-in-a-lifetime event. You must do it many times and in many different ways. And it certainly does not become easier.

The Search for Affection

(Thursday, October 17)

At 9 A.M. I went to Père Thomas for spiritual direction. I asked him about my need for affection. I told him that getting older had not lessened that need, and that I feared it might prevent rather than help the development of my spiritual life. It took me about five minutes to express my problem. Père Thomas responded with a two-hour answer! It was a sermon, a lecture, and an exhortation, as well as a very personal response to my question. After half an hour I was so tired from trying to grasp fully the meaning of his words, as well as his difficult French, that I interrupted him by saying, "Thank you so much, that gives me enough to think about for a long time." But the good Père gave me another hour and a half of profound ideas and insights that will keep me going forever!

At first I felt overwhelmed by this long theological reflection, but now I realize that Père Thomas wanted to help me to think differently before helping me to feel differently. I will try to write down here at least some of his thoughts.

He started by saying that, for many of us in this highly psychologized culture, affection has become the central concern. We have come to judge ourselves in terms of the affection that is given or refused to us. The media—television, radio, magazines, and advertisements—have strongly reinforced the idea that human affection is what we really need. Being loved, liked, appreciated, praised, acknowledged, recognized, etc.—these are the most desired prizes of life. The lack of these forms of affection can throw us into an abyss of loneliness and depression, and even lead us to suicide. We have developed great sophistication in analyzing the many nuances of our affections and developed a rich language which allows us to express how we feel about ourselves and others at different times and in different situations. We have become highly developed psychological beings, and the range of our emotions and feelings regarding personal and interpersonal experiences has become increasingly wide.

I very much agree with Père Thomas's viewpoint. During my years at Harvard, much was said about the giving of love in its many expressions, as well as about the withholding of love through anger, resentment, and indignation. But the highly nuanced psychological language used, even at the divinity school, made spiritual and theological language sound irrelevant, superficial, and even offensive.

But it is precisely this highly developed psychological consciousness that sometimes prevents us from reaching that place in us where the healing powers are hidden. Père Thomas's greatest gift, as I see it, is his ability to speak about that place and mobilize its hidden gifts. He calls that place the heart.

Tomorrow I will try to write down some of his thoughts about the heart.

The Heart

(Friday, October 18)

What is the heart? It is the place of trust, a trust that can be called faith, hope, or love, depending on how it is being manifested. Père

Thomas sees the trusting heart as the most important characteris-
tic of the human person. It is not so much the ability to think, to
reflect, to plan, or to produce that makes us different from the rest
of creation, but the ability to trust. It is the heart that makes us
truly human.

This vital observation helps explain why we respond with our
hearts to our surroundings long before our consciences are developed. Our consciences, which allow us to distinguish between
good and evil and thus give us a basis for moral choice, are less in
control than our hearts. Père Thomas is convinced that much of
the crisis in the life of the Church today is connected with a lack of
knowledge of the heart. Much Church discussion today focuses on
the morality of human behavior: premarital sex, divorce, homosexuality, birth control, abortion, and so on. Many people have become disillusioned with the Church because of these issues. But
when the moral life gets all the attention, we are in danger of
forgetting the primacy of the mystical life, which is the life of the
heart.

Quite often the suggestion is made that the mystical life, a life
in which we enter into a unifying communion with God, is the
highest fruit and most precious reward of the moral life. The
classical distinctions among the purifying way, the illuminating
way, and the unifying way as the three progressively higher levels
of the spiritual life have strengthened this suggestion. Thus we
have come to see the mystical life as the life of the happy few who
reach the prayer of total surrender.

The greatest insight of Père Thomas—an insight in which the
best of his theology and the best of his pastoral experience with
handicapped people merge—is that the mystical life lies at the
beginning of our existence and not just at its end. We are born in
intimate communion with the God who created us in love. We
belong to God from the moment of our conception. Our heart is
that divine gift which allows us to trust not just God, but also our
mother, our father, our family, ourselves, and the world. Père
Thomas is convinced that very small children have a deep, intu-
itive knowledge of God, a knowledge of the heart, that sadly is
often obscured and even suffocated by the many systems of

thought we gradually cultivate. Handicapped people, who have such a limited ability to learn, can let their hearts speak easily and thus reveal a mystical life that for many intelligent people seems unreachable.

By speaking about the heart as the deepest source of the spiritual life, the life of faith, hope, and love, Père Thomas wanted to show me that human affections do not lead us where our hearts want to lead us. The heart is much wider and deeper than our affections. It is before and beyond the distinctions between sorrow and joy, anger and lust, fear and love. It is the place where all is one in God, the place where we truly belong, the place from which we come and to which we always yearn to return.

I now realize that my "simple" question about my affections required a fuller response than I had expected. I need to relearn the central place of the mystical experience in human life.

The Three Monks of Tolstoy

(Saturday, October 19)

This afternoon Maria and Louis Tersteeg, friends of mine from Holland, came to Trosly for an afternoon. It was a joy to see them both. We lunched at La Ferme, prayed for a moment in L'Oratoire, had a short visit with Madame Vanier, enjoyed tea with the people at La Forestière, went to Mass with the whole community, and had dinner at Le Val Fleuri, one of the largest and oldest foyers of L'Arche.

Both Maria and Louis were deeply impressed with what they saw and heard. In many ways L'Arche was an eye-opener for them. When we went back to the station in Compiègne, Louis said, "What I will remember most is the three servers during the Eucharist." Maria fully agreed. Seeing three handicapped men in white albs come close to the altar to help Père Thomas prepare the gifts somehow summarized for them the meaning of all they had seen that afternoon.

"They remind me of the three monks in the Tolstoy story," Louis said. As we talked more, the story came back to life:

Three Russian monks lived on a faraway island. Nobody ever went there, but one day their bishop decided to make a pastoral visit. When he arrived he discovered that the monks didn't even know the Lord's Prayer. So he spent all his time and energy teaching them the "Our Father" and then left, satisfied with his pastoral work. But when his ship had left the island and was back in the open sea, he suddenly noticed the three hermits walking on the water—in fact, they were running after the ship! When they reached it they cried, "Dear Father, we have forgotten the prayer you taught us." The bishop, overwhelmed by what he was seeing and hearing, said, "But, dear brothers, how then do you pray?" They answered, "Well, we just say, 'Dear God, there are three of us and there are three of you, have mercy on us!'" The bishop, awestruck by their sanctity and simplicity, said, "Go back to your island and be at peace."

When Louis saw the three handicapped altar servers, this story came immediately to his mind. Like the three monks of Tolstoy, these men may not be able to remember much, but they can be holy enough to walk on water. And that says much about L'Arche.

6

Feeling the Pain

John's Death

(Thursday, October 24)

My dear friend Rose just called from Oakland, California, to tell me that her son John died yesterday morning at 9:30 A.M. Her voice was full of pain and desolation. "It is so hard, so hard, so hard to keep believing in the midst of all this," she said. "I feel more lost and in anguish than when Dan [her husband] died." I heard her cries, her deep feeling of aloneness, her desperation.

But she also spoke words of consolation: "Oh, Henri, the people of the hospice were so good, loving, and caring. Many are gay or lesbian, and few are part of any church or believe in God, but their love for Johnny was so beautiful, so deep, so generous. Many give up their jobs just to be with their dying brothers and sisters . . . Johnny has been loved to the end . . . I just want you to know." Her words were like drops of hope in a sea of despair, inklings of gratitude in the midst of an overwhelming feeling of loss, flashes of light in a deep darkness.

I said, "Johnny loved you so much and he told me how much your love for him meant to him. Hold on to that. Your pain is deep because you suffered that long journey toward death with him. You and he were so open with each other. You didn't hide anything from each other. You saw and felt his struggle and he saw and felt yours . . . It will be hard for you . . . very hard . . . but I know your love is strong and beautiful."

I didn't know John very well, but a few years ago when I was in San Francisco, Rose introduced me to him and we spent some time together. John told me about his homosexuality and his life in the San Francisco gay community. He did not try to defend his way of living or apologize for it. I remember his great compassion for the people he spoke about, but also his critical remarks about snobbism and capitalism in the San Francisco gay community. He himself was extremely generous. He gave much of his time, money, and energy to people in need and asked very little for himself. Seldom have I known anyone who was so eager to have me understand and learn. He was so nonjudgmental, self-possessed, and honest that I came to think of him as an example of a just man.

Last February, Rose called me in Cambridge to tell me that John was very sick with AIDS. I immediately flew to San Francisco and spent a day with Rose at her home and with John and his friend Mike in the hospital. John asked me to read the Twenty-third Psalm with him. It was the psalm he remembered, the psalm his father had prayed with him. It was a psalm that gave him peace. We prayed the words together several times:

> *The Lord is my shepherd,*
> *there is nothing I shall want.*
> *Fresh and green are the pastures*
> *where he gives me repose.*
> *Near restful waters he leads me*
> *to revive my drooping spirit.*

Tomorrow I want to write a little more about my visit to Rose and John.

John's Agony

(Friday, October 25)

My time with John and Rose showed me the ravaging power of
AIDS. John could hardly stay quiet for a minute. Like a wild
animal caught in a cage, he could find no rest, and his whole body
moved in pain. To see his agony and not be able to do anything, to
know that he would only get worse, was nearly intolerable. But I
was struck by the care which surrounded him. Many AIDS patients are rejected by family and friends. But Rose's love for her
son grew stronger every day of his illness. No condemnation, no
accusation, no rejection, but love as only a mother can give. And
Mike, John's companion, gave every minute of his time and every
ounce of his energy to his sick friend. No complaints, no signs of
irritation, just faithful presence.

Mike knew that John would die soon. But it could be a week, a
month, a year, or longer. He wanted only one thing: for John to
feel a little better and be comfortable during the time that was left
to him. "I don't believe in God," Mike said, "but if John wants to
pray with you, please pray with him. Do anything that is good for
John. That's all that matters to me."

After I returned to Cambridge John began to recover somewhat. He left the hospital and found a small apartment where he
could live with Mike. People from the hospice came daily to care
for John while Mike went to work.

In August I saw John again. He was less restless but suffered
from terrible dizziness. "I want to die," he said. "I cannot bear this
dizziness any longer." I asked him to accept death when it came,
and not to hasten it. We spoke about Rose's and Mike's love and
how much he meant to them. "Try to live for them as long as God
wants you to," I said.

He asked me to give him the sacrament of the sick—"the last

rites," as he called them. He said, "I was baptized and received my First Communion, and I also want to receive the last rites before I die. Will you give me the sacrament?" He wanted to be alone with me. We sat together at the kitchen table. We prayed the Twenty-third Psalm again. I blessed him, crossed his forehead and hands with sacred oil, and prayed for healing—but also for the grace to die with Christ. Together we said, "Our Father, who art in heaven, hallowed be thy name. Thy kingdom come. Thy will be done on earth as it is in heaven."

He said, "Thank you very much," and added in his typical understated way, "This certainly can't hurt me." Afterwards I talked with Mike for a moment. "I am afraid he won't live into the next year," Mike said. "I can't even imagine what it will mean to be without him." I saw Mike's deep suffering. All the attention was on John, but Mike needed support, too. Rose knew this and gave him all she could.

When Rose called me yesterday, she said, "Mike and I cried the whole afternoon yesterday. We had to. I am so glad that Mike and I can support each other. We both miss him so much."

Today John is being cremated. Tuesday there will be a memorial service. Rose will be there. Mike will be there, and so will most of John's brothers and sisters. I will miss being with them. "Can I do something?" I asked Rose on the phone. "If you wish, send some money to the San Francisco hospice people for their work. When they came to help me wash and anoint John's body and take him away, they told us that Johnny was the fourth person to die from AIDS that day in San Francisco. These people are so loving, so caring, so good . . . they may not all believe in God, but they surely help me to do so."

I thank God for having known John and having come to know in a new way the inexhaustible mystery of human suffering and human love.

Seeing Christ

(Saturday, October 26)

For a week now, I have been trying to write a meditation about the icon of Christ the Savior painted by Andrew Rublev. I have not yet been able to write a word, but in fact have experienced an increasing anxiety. I looked at some books on iconography, studied some articles on Rublev's particular style, read through Ian Wilson's book on the Turin Shroud, and let my mind make all sorts of connections but could not find words for writing. I feel tired, even exhausted, because I have spent much mental energy but have found no way to channel it creatively.

I am gradually realizing that what restrains me is the direct confrontation with the face of Jesus. I have written about Rublev's icon of the Trinity and about the icon of Our Lady of Vladimir. Yet writing about the icon of Christ's sacred face is such an awesome undertaking that I wonder if I can really do it.

This afternoon I just looked at this seemingly indescribable icon. I looked at the eyes of Jesus and saw his eyes looking at me. I choked, closed my eyes, and started to pray. I said, "O my God, how can I write about your face? Please give me the words to say what can be said." I read in the Gospels and realized how much is written there about seeing and being seen, about being blind and receiving new sight, and about eyes—human eyes and the eyes of God.

I know I must write about Rublev's icon of Christ because it touches me more than any icon I have ever seen. I must come to know what happens to me when I look at and pray with it. One thing is certain: I have read enough about it. I must simply be present to it, and pray and look and pray and wait and pray and trust. I hope that the right words will come, because if they do, perhaps many will begin to see with me and be touched by those eyes.

A Prayer to See and Be Seen

(Monday, October 28)

O Lord Jesus, I look at you, and my eyes are fixed on your eyes. Your eyes penetrate the eternal mystery of the divine and see the glory of God. They are also the eyes that saw Simon, Andrew, Nathanael, and Levi, the eyes that saw the woman with a hemorrhage, the widow of Nain, the blind, the lame, the lepers, and the hungry crowd, the eyes that saw the sad, rich ruler, the fearful disciples on the lake, and the sorrowful women at the tomb. Your eyes, O Lord, see in one glance the inexhaustible love of God and the seemingly endless agony of all people who have lost faith in that love and are like sheep without a shepherd.

As I look into your eyes, they frighten me because they pierce like flames of fire my innermost being, but they console me as well, because these flames are purifying and healing. Your eyes are so severe yet so loving, so unmasking yet so protecting, so penetrating yet so caressing, so profound yet so intimate, so distant yet so inviting.

I gradually realize that I want to be seen by you, to dwell under your caring gaze, and to grow strong and gentle in your sight. Lord, let me see what you see—the love of God and the suffering of people—so that my eyes may become more and more like yours, eyes that can heal wounded hearts.

Not Milk, but Solid Food

(Tuesday, October 29)

Every Tuesday night I celebrate the Eucharist for the English-speaking assistants of the community. We gather in the small chapel of La Forestière. Not all the English-speaking people can come, but the chapel is quickly filled, especially since a few of the assistants bring a handicapped housemate with them.

I have noticed that these people have little desire for dialogue or discussion, though they do like to pray together, sing together, be silent together, and listen together to a reflection on the Gospel. The assistants are often tired from a long day of work with handicapped men and women, and they want to be nurtured, supported, and cared for.

I must learn a new style of ministry. Few of those who participate in these Tuesday night liturgies need to be convinced of the importance of the Gospels, the centrality of Jesus, or the value of the sacraments. Most have moved beyond that stage. They have discovered Christ; they have made their decision to work with the poor; they have chosen the narrow path.

I still spend much energy convincing them of God's love, calling them to community, and offering them a place to experience the peace of Jesus. That kind of ministry is appropriate in a secular university, where students are fully caught up in the race for achievement. But here there is no urge to success; here time is filled with dressing, feeding, carrying, and just being with those in need. It is a very demanding and tiring way, but there is no rivalry, no degree to be acquired, no honor to be desired—just faithful service.

I do not want to romanticize the young men and women at L'Arche. I am too aware of their struggles, imperfections, and unfulfilled longings. Still, they have made a choice that few have made. Their need is less to be convinced of the importance of that choice than to find encouragement to continue, new perspectives to keep them from falling into a spiritual "rut," and support to remain faithful to what they have already chosen. What they need, to use the words of the apostle Paul, is not milk, but solid food (1 Corinthians 3:2).

This is a new challenge for me. It requires me to develop the art of "spiritual companionship" with these fellow travelers. I now realize that the Gospel of John was written for men and women like these. It was written for mature spiritual persons who do not want to argue about elementary issues, but who want to be introduced into the mysteries of the divine life. I must truly be a man of prayer to be able to respond to this desire.

Tonight we prayed especially for John. I wished I could be with the many who will gather today in California for the memorial service, to express gratitude for having known him. May he now find the love he searched for with so much pain and agony during his short life.

Cries for Affection

(Thursday, October 31)

The November issue of *Messages des Sécours Catholiques*, a monthly newsletter published by a French Catholic organization for emergency relief, is filled with gripping stories about human loneliness. The headline, which I have also seen printed on a poster hanging in many churches, says, "La solitude, Ça existe. La solidarité aussi," which means "Loneliness exists; solidarity, too!" I am moved to see loneliness described as a form of suffering that afflicts not only poor people, prisoners, and the elderly, but also well-educated young adults. Loneliness is first of all a cry for affection. The many letters received by the Sécours Catholiques agency ask not just for food, shelter, money, or a job, but also, and often with greater urgency, for affection.

One letter writer says: "I have a need for affection, for tenderness, but where can I find that in this indifferent world?" Another says: "I have no friends anymore . . . I ask your help to be able to live again with normal people who don't need drugs or alcohol to exist!" Another: "I need someone to help me. I need someone who loves me . . . without that I feel myself slowly dying." Another: "I have never been looked at or listened to. I do not count anymore, I do not exist anymore."*

Much suffering in our time is caused by this need for affection. An increasing number of people have no home. They live alone in small rooms hidden away in large cities. When they return from work there is nobody to welcome them, kiss them, embrace them, and ask them, "How was your day?" There is nobody to cry with, laugh with, walk with, eat with, or just sit with.

Michel, eighteen years of age, writes, "Let me appear on radio or television so that I can cry out about the pain of young men who have never been loved, who have been shuffled from place to place, who have never known the love of a family."†

This is a cry for a real neighbor, for someone who is willing to be close, who gives not just food, a house, or a job, but the sense of being loved. Where are the people who can offer this closeness to their lonely brothers and sisters?

As I think about these questions, I vividly remember Père Thomas's views about the human need for affection. I agree with his viewpoint that in our psychologized culture, human affection has become a central concern. I also realize more than ever before that a new knowledge of God's unconditional love is needed. But reading these desperate cries for affection, I wonder how this unconditional divine love can be experienced in our media-controlled milieu. One thing is becoming clear to me: God became flesh for us to show us that the way to come in touch with God's love is the human way, in which the limited and partial affection

---

* *Messages* No. 376, November 1984, p. 7.
† *Ibid.*, p. 7.

that people can give offers access to the unlimited and complete love that God has poured into the human heart. God's love cannot be found outside this human affection, even when that human affection is tainted by the brokenness of our time.

7

Forgiving the Hurt

Going Beyond Feelings

(Sunday, November 3)

Tonight Jonas arrived. He came directly from Cambridge and will be here in Trosly for ten days. The depression that hit me when he didn't visit during his September vacation in France has lurked under the surface of my mostly cheerful life.

Jonas's visit is very important to me. It will not be an easy time for me, as I need to find ways to forgive him and deepen our friendship. But I trust that God will help me to go beyond my feelings of rejection and find reconciliation.

Sharing the Gifts

(Tuesday, November 5)

Jonas and I spent the day visiting the community. Because he raised many questions from the perspective of a psychologist, I learned much about L'Arche that I had never considered before. I was also reminded of the centrality of "living L'Arche," that is, living in intimate communion with the handicapped. As elsewhere, work is important, the development of behavioral skills is important, health and education are important—but they are all secondary to a life lived together in a community of love. There are doctors, psychologists, psychiatrists, physical therapists, and nurses, but they are all consultants more than leaders. The professionals are here to help the assistants live with the handicapped in a creative, supportive, and healing way.

It is also important that the handicapped people develop as much physical and emotional independence as possible, but never disregarding community life. The central words here are not "equal rights" but rather "sharing the gifts." The handicapped people are different from their assistants, but within their differences lie gifts which need to be discovered, acknowledged, and shared. The handicapped people and the assistants need each other, though sometimes in different ways. Together they seek to form a true fellowship of the weak, always thanking and praising God for the fragile gift of life.

Good News from Daybreak

(Wednesday, November 6)

Sue Mosteller arrived with good news from Daybreak: Raymond left the intensive care unit, Rose's surgery went well, and both are on their way to recovery. She also brought kind words with her from D.J. and from Ray's family.

With Sue, I experienced great joy at this victory over the power of death and I was reminded of the words of the prophet Ezekiel: "Why die, house of Israel? I take no pleasure in the death of anyone . . . so repent and live" (Ezekiel 18:32).

True Amateurs

(Thursday, November 7)

Jonas and I are having an important week together. We are busy visiting foyers, workshops, and specialists. It feels to me like showing a foreigner my hometown and discovering it myself in the process! Because Jonas raises questions, notices events, and makes comparisons differently from me, he has uncovered a different L'Arche from what I had seen so far.

To Jonas, a psychologist in a large institution for handicapped people, L'Arche is a place where the professional distance that allows people to heal others without getting entangled in their many problems is less visible, even absent. L'Arche might at first seem somewhat amateurish to a professional. Still, the word "amateur" is a word we must recover; it suggests a way to understand the true nature of this distance. The word comes from *amare,* which is Latin for "to love."

Life at L'Arche is built upon love, not simply for handicapped people, but for the God of life revealed to us in Jesus Christ, the rejected man of Nazareth. It is a love based upon the knowledge of the heart, a deep conviction that "nothing, neither death nor life, nor angel, nor prince, nothing that exists, nothing still to come, nor any power or height or depth, nor any created thing can ever come between us and the love of God made visible in Christ Jesus our Lord" (Romans 8:38–39). This love is much more than an emotion or feeling. It is rooted in the fact of God's unlimited love for us. It is this love which allows us to be deeply involved with the suffering of the world without being swallowed up by it. It is this love which enables us to listen to the howls and cries of handicapped people without being possessed by them. It is this love which allows us to be very close without ever losing the distance necessary for us to live healthy, joyful, and peaceful lives.

When our love is rooted in God's love, we can carry the burden of life and discover it to be light. Jesus calls us: "Come to me, all you who labor and are overburdened, and I will give you rest. Shoulder my yoke and learn from me, for I am gentle and humble of heart . . . Yes, my yoke is easy and my burden light" (Matthew 11:28–30). The burden of Jesus is the burden of all human suffering, but when we take on that burden in communion with him, it proves to be light and easy. Personally, I think that living close to handicapped people, as do the L'Arche assistants, is impossible unless one draws upon the love of Christ. Without this love, such a life leads to "burnout." But when this love is deep and strong and constantly nurtured by the community, the handicapped people can become conductors of the vision of that greater love which holds us safely.

Thus a new type of distance develops: not a professional distance, which protects us from getting too close to the world's pain, but a spiritual distance, which allows us to let that pain become a light burden.

Struggling with the Nature of Friendship

(Friday, November 8)

Maintaining spiritual distance is a more personal matter than I realized yesterday. It is essential to the understanding and living of true friendship. Jonas and I are trying to deal with our friendship. In the beginning we touched upon it only indirectly, but in the past few days we have been able to explore our relationship more directly. It is hard for me to speak of my feelings of being rejected or imposed upon, of my desire for affirmation as well as my need for space, of insecurity and mistrust, of fear and love. But as I entered into these feelings, I also discovered the real problem —expecting from a friend what only Christ can give.

I feel so easily rejected. When a friend does not come, a letter is not written, or an invitation not extended, I begin to feel unwanted and disliked. I gravitate toward dark feelings of low self-esteem and become depressed. Once depressed, I tend to interpret even innocent gestures as proofs of my self-chosen darkness, from which it is harder and harder to return. Looking carefully at this vicious cycle of self-rejection and speaking about it directly with Jonas is a good way to start moving in the opposite direction.

Two things happened when Jonas and I spoke. First, he forced me to move out of the center! He too has a life, he too has his struggles, he too has unfulfilled needs and imperfections. As I tried to understand his life, I felt a deep compassion and a desire to comfort and console him. I no longer felt so strongly the need to judge him for not paying enough attention to me. It is so easy to convince yourself that you are the one who needs all the attention. But once you can see the other concretely in his or her life situation, you can step back a bit from yourself and understand that, in a true friendship, two people make a dance.

• Second, I learned afresh that friendship requires a constant willingness to forgive each other for not being Christ and a willingness to ask Christ himself to be the true center. When Christ does not mediate a relationship, that relationship easily becomes demanding, manipulating, oppressive, an arena for many forms of rejection. An unmediated friendship cannot last long; you simply expect too much of the other and cannot offer the other the space he or she needs to grow. Friendship requires closeness, affection, support, and mutual encouragement, but also distance, space to grow, freedom to be different, and solitude. To nurture both aspects of a relationship, we must experience a deeper and more lasting affirmation than any human relationship can offer.

As we struggled with the true nature of our friendship, Jonas and I read Paul's words to the Romans: "We know that by turning everything to their good, God cooperates with all those who love him, with all those whom he has called according to his purpose . . . those he called he justified, and with those he justified he shared his glory" (Romans 8:28–30).

When we truly love God and share in his glory, our relationships lose their compulsive character. We reach out to people not just to receive their affirmation, but also to allow them to participate in the love we have come to know through Jesus. Thus true friendship becomes an expression of a greater love.

It is hard work to remind each other constantly of the truth, but it is worth the effort. Constant mutual forgiveness and a continual openness to the love of God are the disciplines which allow us to grow together in friendship.

The Small Seductions of a Sensual World

(Saturday, November 9)

Today Jonas and I spent an afternoon and an evening in Compiègne. We considered going to Paris but were not fully convinced that riding trains and subways, finding a place to stay, and seeing churches and museums would be the best way to conclude our time together at L'Arche. We decided to go to Compiègne and then see if going on to Paris would be attractive to both of us.

In Compiègne it was market day. Thousands of people were walking through the streets, going from stand to stand, looking, arguing, and buying. Parents with their children, small groups of teenagers, single men and women, and elderly couples had all come to town on Saturday to buy for the holiday (Monday, November 11, is Armistice Day), to do their banking, or just to meet friends and have a good time.

Both Jonas and I were struck by the sharp contrast between our quiet, prayerful week in Trosly and our restless, noisy, busy, and crowded afternoon in town. We felt ourselves being distracted, scattered, pulled away from our center, and drawn into the anonymous life of strangers. After a time of peace and joy lived in community, we both experienced a certain inner restlessness and sadness. It seemed as if the city were tempting us with its sensuality: its many colors, movements, things to buy, and people to look at. Jonas spoke about the return of the "desiring mind" after a period of being among the poor and handicapped in a somewhat desire-free way. Our curiosity, which had left us for a while, returned with new force. We both experienced in the people, movements, and places of Compiègne a temptation to lose touch with God's kingdom and be swept up by desires for the many "other things" (Luke 12:31) of this world.

We were glad we could talk about these things. Often such experiences remain hidden and cause much shame and guilt. But by confessing to each other how easily we are seduced by the attractions of the world, we affirmed our true commitment and safeguarded that commitment in each other. I now understand much better why Jesus sent his disciples into the world in groups of two rather than alone. Together, they could maintain the spirit of peace and love they found in his company and could share these gifts with everyone they met.

After four hours in Compiègne, we decided to return to Trosly and have a quiet, prayerful Sunday there. We weren't ready for Paris yet!

A Forgiven Person Forgives

(Monday, November 11)

Often I am not prepared for my morning meditation and end up just sitting in the oratory at 7 A.M. with all kinds of thoughts except the thought my meditation subject suggests to me.

But I simply must stay with it, even when it seems quite pointless. This morning I meditated on God's eagerness to forgive me, revealed in the words of the One Hundred Third Psalm: "As far as the East is from the West, so far does God remove my sin." In the midst of all my distractions, I was touched by God's desire to forgive me again and again. If I return to God with a repentant heart after I have sinned, God is always there to embrace me and let me start afresh. "The Lord is compassion and love, slow to anger and rich in mercy."

It is hard for me to forgive someone who has really offended me, especially when it happens more than once. I begin to doubt the sincerity of the one who asks forgiveness for a second, third, or fourth time. But God does not keep count. God just waits for our return, without resentment or desire for revenge. God wants us home. "The love of the Lord is everlasting."

Maybe the reason it seems hard for me to forgive others is that I do not fully believe that I am a forgiven person. If I could fully accept the truth that I am forgiven and do not have to live in guilt or shame, I would really be free. My freedom would allow me to forgive others seventy times seven times. By not forgiving, I chain myself to a desire to get even, thereby losing my freedom. A forgiven person forgives. This is what we proclaim when we pray, "and forgive us our trespasses as we forgive those who have trespassed against us."

This lifelong struggle lies at the heart of the Christian life.

Forgiveness and Freedom

(Tuesday, November 12)

Jonas left this morning. I got up early, broke two wine glasses trying to find my way around the kitchen, made Jonas a sandwich for his train ride, and then walked to his room. We prayed together in the oratory, had a quick breakfast, and discovered that Simone had also made him a sandwich for the train. Barbara picked us up in one of the L'Arche Renaults and drove us to the station. The train to Brussels appeared on the minute. We embraced, said good words to each other, and waved good-bye as the train pulled away. Barbara said, "He is a very nice man. It was good for us that he came. I hope it was also good for him."

Tonight, during the Eucharist for the English-speaking assistants, we heard the words of Jesus: "Forgive your brother from your heart." I spoke about the freedom that forgiveness can bring, and many people said afterwards that my words had touched them deeply. I discovered once again that what is most personal is most universal. Jonas had left, but his leaving was a good leaving that was already bearing fruit.

8

Jesus in the Center

Be Faithful in Your Adoration

(Friday, November 15)

Father George Strohmeyer, the co-founder of L'Arche community in Erie, Pennsylvania, is visiting for a few weeks. This morning I had a chance to speak with him about being a priest for
L'Arche.

He told me about his "conversion" when he came to Trosly for
the first time. His hours of adoration in front of the Blessed Sacrament and his contacts with Père Thomas were the two main
causes behind his more radical turn to Jesus. As he told his story, it
became clear that Jesus is at the center of his life. This would seem
obvious for a priest, but such is not always the case. George has
come to know Jesus in a way few priests have. When he pronounces the name of Jesus you know that he speaks from a deep,
intimate encounter. His life has become simpler, more hidden,
more rooted, more trusting, more open, more evangelical, and
more peaceful. For George, being a priest at L'Arche means lead-

ing people—the handicapped and their assistants—always closer to Jesus.

I now know for sure that there is a long, hard journey ahead of me. It is the journey of leaving everything behind for Jesus' sake. I now know that there is a way of living, praying, being with people, caring, eating, drinking, sleeping, reading, and writing in which Jesus is truly the center. I know from Jean Vanier, from Père Thomas, and from the many assistants who live here that this way exists and that I have not fully found it yet.

How do I find it? George gave me the answer: "Be faithful in your adoration." He did not say "prayer" or "meditation" or "contemplation." He kept using the word "adoration." This word makes it clear that all the attention must be on Jesus and not on me. To adore is to be drawn away from my own preoccupations into the presence of Jesus. It means letting go of what I want, desire, and have planned and fully trusting Jesus and his love.

Talking to George creates a certain jealousy in me. It seems as if he stands on the other side of the river and calls me to jump in and swim. But I am afraid; I think I will drown. I think I am not prepared to let go of all the good things on my side of the river. But I also want to be where he is; I sense the freedom, joy, and peace he has found. There is a clarity about him that I lack, an utter simplicity, a total commitment, and a vision that do not come from reading or studying but are a gift from God. I am jealous but also ambivalent, hesitant, and doubting. There is a voice in me that says, "You don't want to become a fanatic, a sectarian, a Jesus freak, a narrow-minded enthusiast . . . you want to remain open to many ways of being, explore many options, be informed about many things . . ." I know that this is not the voice I should trust. It is the voice that keeps me from making a full commitment to Jesus and from truly seeing the way God wants me to be in the world.

To give, not from my wealth but from my want, as the widow of Jerusalem who donated her last coin, that is the great challenge of the Gospel. When I look critically at my life, I find that my generosity always occurs in the context of great wealth. I give some of my money, some of my time, some of my energy, and some of my thoughts to God and others, but enough money, time,

energy, and thoughts always remain to maintain my own security.
Thus I never really give God a chance to show me his boundless
love.

Maybe following George's example is the best I can do: ador-
ing Jesus in the Blessed Sacrament every day, listening more to
Père Thomas, and consistently choosing a life among the poor.

Returning with an Impure Heart

(Sunday, November 17)

For three days I have been meditating on the story of the prodigal
son. It is a story about returning. I realize the importance of returning over and over again. My life drifts away from God. I have
to return. My heart moves away from my first love. I have to
return. My mind wanders to strange images. I have to return.
Returning is a lifelong struggle.

It strikes me that the wayward son had rather selfish motivations. He said to himself, "How many of my father's paid servants
have more food than they want, and here am I dying of hunger! I
will leave this place and go to my father." He didn't return because of a renewed love for his father. No, he returned simply to
survive. He had discovered that the way he had chosen was leading him to death. Returning to his father was a necessity for staying
alive. He realized that he had sinned, but this realization came
about because sin had brought him close to death.

I am moved by the fact that the father didn't require any
higher motivation. His love was so total and unconditional that he
simply welcomed his son home.

This is a very encouraging thought. God does not require a
pure heart before embracing us. Even if we return only because
following our desires has failed to bring happiness, God will take us
back. Even if we return because being a Christian brings us more

peace than being a pagan, God will receive us. Even if we return because our sins did not offer as much satisfaction as we had hoped, God will take us back. Even if we return because we could not make it on our own, God will receive us. God's love does not require any explanations about why we are returning. God is glad to see us home and wants to give us all we desire, just for being home.

In my mind's eye I see Rembrandt's painting *The Return of the Prodigal Son.* The dim-eyed old father holds his returned son close to his chest with an unconditional love. Both of his hands, one strong and masculine, the other gentle and feminine, rest on his son's shoulders. He does not look at his son but feels his young, tired body and lets him rest in his embrace. His immense red cape is like the wings of a mother bird covering her fragile nestling. He seems to think only one thing: "He is back home, and I am so glad to have him with me again."

So why delay? God is standing there with open arms, waiting to embrace me. He won't ask any questions about my past. Just having me back is all he desires.

A Jealous Love

(Monday, November 18)

I am growing in the awareness that God wants my whole life, not just part of it. It is not enough to give just so much time and attention to God and keep the rest for myself. It is not enough to pray often and deeply and then move from there to my own projects.

As I try to understand why I am still so restless, anxious, and tense, it occurs to me that I have not yet given everything to God. I notice this especially in my greediness for time. I am very concerned to have enough hours to develop my ideas, finish my projects, fulfill my desires. Thus, my life is in fact divided into two parts, a part for God and a part for myself. Thus divided, my life cannot be peaceful.

To return to God means to return to God with all that I am and all that I have. I cannot return to God with just half of my being. As I reflected this morning again on the story of the prodigal son and tried to experience myself in the embrace of the father, I suddenly felt a certain resistance to being embraced so fully and totally. I experienced not only a desire to be embraced, but also a fear of losing my independence. I realized that God's love is a jealous love. God wants not just a part of me, but all of me. Only when I surrender myself completely to God's parental love can I expect to be free from endless distractions, ready to hear the voice of love, and able to recognize my own unique call.

It is going to be a very long road. Every time I pray, I feel the struggle. It is the struggle of letting God be the God of my whole being. It is the struggle to trust that true freedom lies hidden in total surrender to God's love.

Following Jesus is the way to enter into the struggle and find true freedom. The way is the way of the cross, and true freedom is the freedom found in the victory over death. Jesus' total obedience to his Father led him to the cross, and through the cross to a life no longer subject to the competitive games of this world. Jesus held on to nothing, not even to satisfying religious experiences. His words "My God, my God, why have you forsaken me?" give us a glimpse of the complete surrender of Jesus to his Father. Nothing was left for him to cling to. In this complete surrender he found total unity and total freedom.

To me Jesus says, "Come and follow me . . . I have come so that you may have life and have it abundantly" (John 10:10).

Searching for the Right Words

(Thursday, November 28)

Words, words, words! Tonight we start a "reflection weekend." All day I have been looking in the dictionary to find the French words for a talk I must give tomorrow to all the assistants of the community.

I am also struggling to find a way to maintain some spontaneity while speaking in a foreign language. My desire to make no mistakes can inhibit my freedom of expression. But too many mistakes are distracting and prevent people from hearing the message.

My main problem, however, is on a much deeper level. How do I speak to people whom I perceive to be more converted than I am? I have been asked to speak about hope in the midst of a world full of despair. But what can I say about hope to people whose lives are a living proof of hope? The 250 assistants here at L'Arche have left home, career, and wealth in order to live simple lives with people who are considered useless by the world. This is certainly a radical way of proclaiming hope.

So I feel as if I am carrying coals to Newcastle or, as the Dutch say, "bringing owls to Athens" or, as the French say, "bringing water to the river." But whatever expression you use, it is hard to speak well to the converted! I know I must speak because I have been asked to speak, and proclaiming the Good News is my vocation. In this case, I trust that those who will be listening tomorrow will be able to hear beyond my limping words, will be affirmed in the choices they have already made, and will help me to believe so strongly in my own words that I will find new courage to put them into practice. Occasionally the main fruit of speaking is the conversion of the speaker!

With that hope I can go ahead and let my words do the work for me.

A True Experience of Church

(Friday, November 29)

The reflection weekend is a unique event at L'Arche since it is the only time during the year when the assistants gather without the handicapped people and reflect on their life at L'Arche. It is a retreat, but also a celebration. It is a time to pray, sing, and think, but also a time to get to know each other and feel part of one body.

Because the foyers are spread across four different villages and the assistants must be home most of the time, you never realize how many people work at L'Arche. But last night, during the opening of the reflection weekend, I was struck by how large the community really is. At least 250 men and women came together—young, old, married and single, coming from the most diverse places in the world to be with the poor in spirit. A festive mood prevailed, and everyone was happy to have these days to be together. Most of the handicapped men and women have gone home or to their "special families" so that the assistants can receive all the attention for a change.

I am coming to realize how generous these people, who usually remain hidden in their busy homes with their broken brothers and sisters, really are. As we were together talking, laughing, singing, and praying, I experienced church in the best sense of that word: a people called together to praise God and to serve the poor.

My presentation this morning was well received. Much better than I expected. Nobody seemed to have problems understanding my French, and most people felt that what I said was clear and helped them in their discussions. I spoke about the movement from despair to hope. I described despair as it is visible in interpersonal relationships, in the world at large, and in the Church and I discussed how prayer, resistance, and community are three aspects of a life of hope in the midst of a despairing world.

I feel grateful for the warm response of the assistants. It makes me feel more a part of this community and gives me a sense of having made a small contribution to people who have given me so much.

9

The Important and the Urgent

Making Closer Connections

(Saturday, November 30)

The most important event of the day for me was the arrival of my coworker Peter Weiskel. Peter flew from Boston to Brussels this morning and arrived in Compiègne by train at 7 P.M. It is great to have him here for two weeks. Working together with such a great distance between us has not always been easy. And though we have regular contact by letter and phone, our communication is often difficult and at times frustrating. It is hard for Peter to envision my daily life here in France and to feel fully a part of the situations I am describing in this journal. I hope that his two weeks here will make him feel more connected to L'Arche and more able to help me think through some of the concerns I am writing about while here.

The First Gothic Arch!

(Sunday, December 1)

This afternoon Peter and I attended Vespers in the church of Our Lady of Morienval. Morienval is a small village about a half hour's drive from Trosly.

We were not prepared for this unusual event. About thirty people sang Vespers together for the first Sunday of Advent. Most of them were members of religious orders from the area. The pastor who had organized the simple service told us that no Vespers had been sung in that church since 1745, when the Benedictine sisters, whose abbey church it was, left the area. It was a moving experience to pray with this small group of believers. We reached out over the centuries to those who had preceded us and took up the prayer that had been interrupted for 240 years.

This in itself was unusual enough. But when the service was over and we had a chance to look around, we realized that we had come upon one of the most precious architectural gems in France. Built around 1050 in fine Romanesque style, the church has a central nave, three aisles, and a majestic clock tower. Its wide transepts and semicircular choir are flanked by two elegant, decorative towers. Compared to a cathedral, it is a small, homely church. We were astonished to see an eleventh-century church in such a fine state of preservation. Neither the feudal conflicts of the Middle Ages, nor the French Revolution, nor the First and Second World Wars had done any harm to it. It is undoubtedly one of the best-preserved Romanesque churches in France.

The pastor of the church was eager to tell us about its history. He took us to the apse and showed us that one of the arches was pointed, in contrast to the rounded curves of the other Romanesque arches. As if he were betraying a secret, he whispered, "It is said that this is the first Gothic arch in the world." I was quite impressed to stand at the birthplace of the Gothic style, which would dominate the next several centuries. As a whole, the church was still round, down-to-earth, and simple. But the builder had begun to express an urge to go higher and strive for the heavens!

The pastor turned on all the lights in the church and let the tower bells ring. Suddenly all was light and sound. We felt privileged to have a glimpse of the devotion and faith of people who had lived nine hundred years before us. They sang the same psalms as we did and prayed to the same Lord as we did. We felt once again a joyful, hope-giving connection with the past.

As we left the church, a group of teenagers with a loud portable radio walked through the square, calling us back to the twentieth century. But as we looked at the church again and realized the beauty of this house of prayer, we said to each other, "We really should come back here and pray Vespers again." It seemed the right thing to do. The church was built for prayer.

Our Fragmented Lives

(Monday, December 2)

Not much to report today except for many little frustrations, interruptions, and distractions. One of those days that pass without having felt like a real day. Many letters, telephone calls, short visits, little talks, but no real work, no sense of moving, no sense of direction. A day that is so fragmented that it does not seem to come together at all—except perhaps by writing about it!

One of the great gifts of the spiritual life is to know that even days like this are not a total waste. There was still an hour of prayer. There was still the Eucharist, there were still moments of gratitude for the gifts of life. And there is the opportunity to realize that a day like this unites me with thousands, even millions, of people for whom many days are like this, yet who are in no position to do anything about it. So many men, women, and children dream about creative lives; yet because they are not free to shape their own lives, they cannot realize their dreams. I had better pray for them tonight.

Choosing What Is Important

(Tuesday, December 3)

This morning I spoke with Père André about my restlessness. Père André is a Jesuit priest from Belgium who spends part of the year at Trosly. He directs the Jesuits who make their third year of formation at L'Arche and gives spiritual guidance to many of the assistants. I told him I have the sense of being terribly busy without really feeling that I am moving down the right path. Père André responded by saying that I have to keep a careful eye on the difference between urgent things and important things. If I allow the urgent things to dominate my day, I will never do what is truly important and will always feel dissatisfied. He said, "You will always be surrounded by urgent things. That is part of your character and your way of living. You move from Harvard to Trosly to get away from the busy life, and soon Trosly is as busy for you as Harvard. The issue is not where you are, but how you live wherever you are. For you that means a constant choosing of what is important and a willingness to accept that the urgent things can wait or be left undone."

I know both how right this advice is and how difficult it is for me to put it into practice. I responded, "How do I know what to let go of? Should I not answer my mail, not write that book, not visit or receive these persons, not pray, not spend so much time with handicapped people? What is urgent and what is important?" He said, "You have to decide to whom you want to be obedient."

We talked about the question of obedience a bit. Then he said, "Why don't you let me be your authority. Stop writing books and articles for a while, answer your mail, be good to those who visit you, pray, and just be here at L'Arche without worrying so much."

When I came home, I felt a lot freer. I started to answer letters and felt good about spending my time this way. I could even say to myself, "You are not allowed to do anything else!" My restlessness faded as I went about my work.

The Knowledge of the Heart

(Wednesday, December 4)

Tonight I was invited to the Oasis foyer to participate in the weekly house meeting and supper. It was a special evening since Daniel, a handicapped man in the foyer, had just learned that his father had died. It requires special care and attention to offer consolation and support to people who express themselves with so much difficulty. The assistants at Oasis wondered how to guide Daniel through this time of grief.

During the house meeting Daniel was the center of attention for a long time. He spoke with difficulty about his grandmother, whose grief over her son's death had touched him deeply. People listened to him with much attention and love. Then Daniel made a surprising proposal. He invited all the members of the foyer to come to his room and pray. This was remarkable since Daniel never joined in evening prayer and was very protective of his privacy. People never just went into his room. But tonight he invited everyone to enter more deeply into his life to be with him in his grief. He placed some candles and small statues on the floor. Pépé, one of the other handicapped men, brought a picture of his deceased mother and put it next to the candles and the statues. I was deeply moved by this gesture of solidarity in grief. Pépé had little to say, but by putting his own mother's photograph on the floor of Daniel's room, he said more than any of us could with our sympathetic words.

The twelve of us huddled together in Daniel's small bedroom and prayed for him, his father, his mother, his grandmother, and his friends. We showed him a picture of Jesus and asked him who it was. "It is Jesus, the hidden one," he answered. For Daniel, Jesus was hard to reach, but tonight this small group of friends made Jesus more tangible than ever before.

As one of the assistants drove me home, she said, "We were worrying about how to help Daniel, but he himself showed us a way nobody else would ever have thought of. The heart knows so much more than the mind!"

Happy Are the Poor

(Thursday, December 5)

Jean Vanier gave a short talk last Sunday morning at the conclusion of the reflection weekend. He said some things then that have stayed with me the whole week. I now realize that what he said has a special meaning for me, and that I must not let it pass as just another beautiful talk.

Three thoughts have stayed with me. First, Jean said that working and living with handicapped people does not become easier the longer you do it. In fact, it often becomes harder. Jean shared his own struggle with us. He said, "Often I go off in dreams about living and being with the poor, but what the poor need are not my dreams, my beautiful thoughts, my inner reflections, but my concrete presence. There is always the temptation to replace real presence with lovely thoughts about being present."

Second, Jean remarked that we have to move from feelings to conviction. As long as our relationship with handicapped people rests on feelings and emotions, a long-term, lifelong commitment cannot develop. In order to stay with the handicapped even when we do not feel like staying, we need a deep conviction that God has called us to be with the poor, whether that gives us good or bad feelings. Jean expressed gratitude toward the many people who come to L'Arche for a month, six months, or a year. He said it was important for them and for L'Arche. But what is most needed are people who have come to the conviction that they are called to be with the handicapped permanently. This conviction makes a covenant possible, a lasting bond with the poor.

Finally, Jean said that poverty is neither nice nor pleasant. Nobody truly wants to be poor. We all want to move away from poverty. And still . . . God loves the poor in a special way. I was deeply struck with Jean's remark: "Jesus did not say, 'Happy are those who serve the poor,' but 'Happy are the poor.' " Being poor is what Jesus invites us to, and that is much, much harder than serving the poor. The unnoticed, unspectacular, unpraised life in solidarity with people who cannot give anything that makes us feel important is far from attractive. It is the way to poverty. Not an easy way, but God's way, the way of the cross.

These three themes have had a deep impact upon me. God is speaking to me in a way that I cannot just pass by. Jean's thoughts are much more than thoughts for me. They are important themes to consider in my own process of discerning a new direction.

10

Poverty and Wealth

Monastic Life

(Paris; Friday, December 6)

Since this is Peter's first visit to Europe, it seemed good to see more than just the little village of Trosly and its surrounding villages. So we decided to spend a day and a half in Paris, enjoy the beauty of this great city, and get a sense of its spiritual life. Tonight we attended Vespers and Mass at the Church of St. Gervais, undoubtedly one of the most remarkable centers of new religious vitality in France.

St. Gervais is the spiritual home of the Monastic Fraternities of Jerusalem. These parallel communities of men and women have chosen the city as their place of prayer, in contrast to the great contemplative orders of the past, which built their monasteries and abbeys in the peaceful countryside.

Being in St. Gervais and praying with the monks and nuns and the several hundred Parisians who had come directly from their work to the service was a deeply moving experience for both Peter and me. The liturgy was both festive and solemn, a real expression of adoration. The monks and nuns wore flowing white robes. The music had a prayerful, polyphonic quality reminiscent of Byzantine rites. There were icons, candles, and incense. People sat on the floor or on small benches. The atmosphere was very quiet, harmonious, prayerful, and peaceful. To come from the busy, restless city streets into the large church, and to be embraced by the simple splendor of the liturgy, was an experience that made a deep impression on both of us.

Peter picked up a flyer describing the spirituality of the brothers and sisters of Jerusalem. There I read:

Life in the city today is a wilderness for the masses of men and women who live alone, some worrying about the future, some unconcerned, each unknown to the other. The brothers and sisters of Jerusalem want to live in solidarity with them, just as they are now, and wherever they are. They wish to provide them with some kind of oasis, freely open to all, a silent place alive with prayer, in a spirit of welcome and sharing, where real life means more than mere talking or acting. A peaceful place where all people, whatever their social background, their age, or their outlook on life, are invited to come and share in a common search for God.

At St. Gervais, we found what these words describe. I have often thought about the possibility of living a truly contemplative life in the heart of the city. Is it possible? Or just a romantic dream? At Cambridge I had tried to start something like that among my students. But my own busyness, restlessness, and inner tension showed that I was not yet ready for it. I needed much more inner discipline than I could develop at a highly demanding university. But the Brothers and Sisters of Jerusalem are doing it. Their self-description continues:

They have chosen to live in Paris, that large city made up of ten million people. Through their own experience of the hardships of city life, with its alienations, its struggles, its work, its restraints, they know the stress, the noise of pollution, the joys and the sorrows, the sinfulness, and the holiness of Paris. Together with the people of Paris, they would like to help point out "the signs announcing the kingdom" in a very humble way, but wholeheartedly, at once breaking off with the world and living in communion with it, both keeping apart and sharing with others . . . They choose to be neither Benedictines nor Trappists, nor Carmelites nor Dominicans. They are "city folk" or, in other words, "monks and nuns of Jerusalem."

When we walked out of the church at 7:30 P.M., looking for a place to eat, we saw some familiar faces: people we had met at L'Arche. I realized that this church has become a home for many people, a place to be together in quiet prayer, a center to form a community, and most of all a *foyer* that makes it possible to live in Babylon while remaining in Jerusalem.

Paris: Rich and Poor

(Saturday, December 7)

As Peter and I walked through Paris today, we were impressed by its abundance as well as by its poverty. The stores, be they bookstores or foodstores, offer a wealth and variety found in few other cities. People throng the city, looking, buying, drinking coffee, having lively conversations, laughing, kissing, and playing.

In the subways, guitarists and singers with portable microphones and loudspeakers join the ride, sing rock songs, and ask for donations. On one train we were treated to a puppet show with a dancing moon, a talking bear, and a sweet melody.

Paris is full of life, movement, art, music, and people of all ages, races, and nationalities. So much is going on—often at the same time—that it is hard not to feel overwhelmed by the enormous variety of impressions. Paris is exhilarating, surprising, exciting, and stimulating, but also very tiring.

We also saw the other side: many poor, hungry people living on the streets, sleeping in subway stations, sitting on church steps begging for money. There are so many unemployed, so many alcoholics, so many drug users, so many mentally and physically ill people that those who want to offer them shelter, food, and counsel can never feel they have finished the task. Amid all the beauty, wealth, and abundance of Paris, there is immense suffering, undeniable loneliness, and unreachable human anguish.

Where Misery and Mercy Meet

(Trosly; Sunday, December 8)

Every Sunday at 5 P.M. it is Jean Vanier's custom to share with the community some of his reflections on the Gospel. But this year his many travels around the world have made this *partage* (sharing) only an occasional event.

But today he was home. Jean sat on the floor of the hall of Les Marronniers, surrounded by about forty people—some handicapped people, some assistants, and quite a few visitors. He read from the Gospel of St. Luke and then meditated aloud on the words he had just read. Being present at this session felt like being invited to enter into the prayer of a friend. No great theological analysis, no difficult words, no complicated ideas—just a faithful penetration of the word of God.

Jean said many things that moved me. But one sentence stayed with me and has continued to grow in me. He said, "Jesus always leads us to littleness. It is the place where misery and mercy meet. It is the place where we encounter God."

Having seen some of the poverty of Paris and having heard Jean say last Sunday that we are called not just to serve the poor but to *be* poor, I was struck forcefully by his words. To choose the little people, the little joys, the little sorrows, and to trust that it is there that God will come close—that is the hard way of Jesus. Again I felt a deep resistance toward choosing that way.

I am quite willing to work for and even with little people, but I want it to be a great event! Something in me always wants to turn the way of Jesus into a way that is honorable in the eyes of the world. I always want the little way to become the big way. But Jesus' movement toward the places the world wants to move away from cannot be made into a success story.

Every time we think we have touched a place of poverty, we will discover greater poverty beyond that place. There is really no way back to riches, wealth, success, acclaim, and prizes. Beyond physical poverty there is mental poverty, beyond mental poverty there is spiritual poverty, and beyond that there is nothing, nothing but the naked trust that God is mercy.

It is not a way we can walk alone. Only with Jesus can we go to the place where there is nothing but mercy. It is the place from which Jesus cried, "My God, my God, why have you forsaken me?" It is also the place from which Jesus was raised up to new life.

The way of Jesus can be walked only with Jesus. If I want to do it alone, it becomes a form of inverse heroism as fickle as heroism itself. Only Jesus, the Son of God, can walk to that place of total surrender and mercy. He warns us about striking off on our own: "cut off from me, you can do nothing." But he also promises, "Whoever remains in me, with me in him, bears fruit in plenty" (John 15:5).

I now see clearly why action without prayer is so fruitless. It is only in and through prayer that we can become intimately connected with Jesus and find the strength to join him on his way.

Seeing and Hearing

(Monday, December 9)

Since Peter's arrival I have been more concerned with seeing than with hearing. One of Peter's reasons for spending two weeks here is to make a photographic essay of life at L'Arche in Trosly. So much can be shown that cannot be said. So much can be expressed by a face that cannot be expressed in words. Among handicapped people words are certainly not the most important way of communicating. Often the eyes say more than the mouth.

Peter has taken hundreds of photographs. He moved gradually from catching the beauty and charm of houses, gates, and statues to catching the more hidden beauty and charm of people playing, laughing, eating, and praying together. He was wise to wait a while before making photographs of the men and women living here in community. A relationship of trust must develop before people are willing to be photographed.

It is remarkable how much easier it is to get permission to make a tape recording than to take a photograph. It seems as if taking a picture is experienced as more of an intrusion than recording a voice. Happily, the people here have become more and more at ease with Peter's presence as a photographer and have even started to invite him to their homes and places of work to take pictures. His kindness and patience have made him seem less and less a threat and more and more a friend. We like to show our faces to our friends.

In the Gospels, "to see" and "to hear" are among the most used words. Jesus says to his disciples, "blessed are your eyes because they see, your ears because they hear! In truth I tell you, many prophets and upright people longed to see what you see, and never saw it; to hear what you hear, and never heard it" (Matthew 13:16–17). Seeing and hearing God are the greatest gifts we can receive. Both are ways of knowing, but all through the scriptures I sense that seeing God is the more intimate and personal of the two. This is confirmed by my own experience. A telephone conversation is such a poor way of being together compared to an encounter face to face. And don't we often say on the phone, "I look forward to seeing you soon"? Seeing is better than hearing. It is a lot closer.

While I try to find words that can be heard or read, Peter tries to find images that can be seen. Few people at L'Arche will read what I write or hear what I say, but many will look again and again at the photographs Peter has made.

Peter's presence here is a great gift—not just to me, but to all who will see what he saw and rejoice in the way he saw it.

The Consolation of Mary

(Tuesday, December 10)

My prayer life has been quite difficult lately. During my morning meditation I think about a thousand things except God and God's presence in my life. I am worrying, brooding, and agonizing, but not really praying.

To my own surprise the only prayer that offers me some peace and consolation is the prayer to Mary. My meditation on the Annunciation brought me real peace and joy, while reflections on other mysteries could not keep me focused. As I tried to simply be with Mary and listen to her words, "You see before you the Lord's servant; let it happen to me as you have said" (Luke 1:38), I discovered a restful peace. Instead of thinking about these words and trying to understand them, I just listened to them being spoken for me.

Mary is so open, so free, so trusting. She is completely willing to hear words that go far beyond her own comprehension. She knows that the words spoken to her by the angel come from God.

She seeks clarification, but she does not question their authority. She senses that the message of Gabriel will radically interrupt her life, and she is afraid, but she does not withdraw. When she hears the words "You will bear a son . . . he will be called the son of the most high," she asks, "But how can this come about, since I have no knowledge of man?" Then she hears what no other human being ever heard: "The Holy Spirit will come upon you and the power of the Most High will cover you with its shadow." She responded with a complete surrender and thus became not only the mother of Jesus but also the mother of all who believe in him. ". . . let it happen to me as you have said" (Luke 1:34–35, 38).

I keep listening to these words as words that summarize the deepest possible response to God's loving action within us. God wants to let the Holy Spirit guide our lives, but are we prepared to let it happen? Just being with Mary and the angel and hearing their words—words which changed the course of history—bring me peace and rest.

I shared this experience with Père André this morning. He said, "Just stay there. Stay with Mary. Trust that she will show you the way. Do not move on as long as you find peace and rest with her. It is clear that she wants your attention. Give it to her, and you will soon understand why it is you are so distracted."

Simple, good, and consoling advice. I do not have to move faster than I can. I have received permission to stay in the place where I am consoled. It is the place where Mary says "Yes" to God's love.

Doing and Being

(Thursday, December 12)

Peter left today. He felt increasingly at ease as he came to know the community. I wished he could have stayed longer. It seemed that the twelve days he was here were not enough to finish all the work, meet all the people, and see all the sights. But I am grateful he came. He now has an idea of life at L'Arche here in Trosly. It will certainly help us a lot in our work together in the year ahead. He can now visualize the situation in which I live, recognize the names of persons about whom I write, and explain to those who come to see him in Cambridge how L'Arche lives and works in France. The more than six hundred photographs he made while here will certainly be helpful in telling the story.

I am a little sad that we had so little time to just be together. There always seemed to be something that needed to be done. Even here, in this quiet, sleepy village, time seems to fly. Friendship is such a holy gift, but we give it so little attention. It is so easy to let what needs to be done take priority over what needs to be lived. Friendship is more important than the work we do together. Both Peter and I know and feel that, but we still don't live it very well.

As the train rolled away from the station, I thought, "He should come back and stay longer, have more time to pray, talk, and just waste time." But I know that I, too, must become a different person to make that happen.

Certainly our time together has deepened our bond and strengthened our love for each other. It is a love that grows by forgiving each other constantly for not yet being who we want to be for each other.

11

A Clear Call

The Call

(Friday, December 13)

Yesterday was not only the day on which Peter left, but also the day on which I received a long letter from Daybreak in Canada inviting me to join their community.

The fact that the letter arrived on the same day that Peter left has a great symbolic meaning for me. On August 15, Peter will conclude his work with me and begin his studies in geology; Joe Egan has invited me to begin living with the Daybreak community on August 29. Something is coming to a conclusion; something new is beginning. I realize that my Cambridge period is ending and that I am being asked to move in a new direction.

Joe writes, "This letter comes to you from the Daybreak Community Council and we are asking you to consider coming to live with us in our community of Daybreak . . . We truly feel that you have a gift to bring us. At the same time, our sense is that Daybreak would be a good place for you, too. We would want to support you in your important vocation of writing and speaking by providing you with a home and with a community that will love you and call you to grow."

I am deeply moved by this letter. It is the first time in my life that I have been explicitly called. All my work as priest since my ordination has been a result of my own initiative. My work at the Menninger Clinic, Notre Dame, Yale, and Harvard and in Latin America has been work that I myself chose. It was mostly very satisfying work, but it was always my own choice. Though I was directly responsible to Cardinal Alfrink and Cardinal Willebrands, and though I am now directly responsible to Cardinal Simonis, none of them has ever called me to a specific task. They have always agreed with and supported the choices I made.

But now a community is saying, "We call you to live with us; to give to us and receive from us." I know that Joe's invitation is not a job offer but a genuine call to come and live with the poor. They have no money to offer, no attractive living quarters, no prestige. This is a completely new thing. It is a concrete call to follow Christ, to leave the world of success, accomplishment, and honor, and to trust Jesus and him alone.

Both the assistants and the handicapped people at Daybreak have been consulted—the call comes from the whole community. It is a call made after much prayer and thought. If I ever wanted a concrete sign of Jesus' will for me, this is it.

I feel many hesitations. Living with handicapped people in a new country is not immediately attractive. Still, something tells me that Joe's letter is not just another letter asking me to do something. It is a response to my prayer to Jesus, asking him where to go. So often I have prayed, "Lord, show me your will and I will do it." So here is a response, more concrete and more specific than I ever dared to hope for.

The coming months will be months to grow into a faithful answer. I must speak to Cardinal Simonis in Holland and ask his permission to accept Joe's call. I must pray for the strength and courage to be truly obedient to Jesus, even if he calls me to where I would rather not go.

Present to the Present

(Wednesday, December 18)

Just a week after I had bought some postcards with reproductions
of paintings by Cézanne, Rainer Maria Rilke's *Letters on Cézanne*
was sent to me as a Christmas gift. It is a happy coincidence. Ever
since I read *Letters to a Young Poet,* I have felt a deep connection
with Rilke. Now he will introduce me to Cézanne, whose paintings
I like but have not yet fully seen. Rilke will help me to see.

When Rilke wrote to his wife, Clara, about Cézanne's painting
of Mont Sainte-Victoire, he said, "Not since Moses has anyone seen
a mountain so greatly . . . only a saint could be as united with his
God as Cézanne was with his work."* For Rilke, Cézanne was
indeed a mystic who helped us to see reality in a new way. He
writes about Cézanne as a painter who "so incorruptibly reduced a
reality to its color content that that reality resumed a new existence in a beyond of color, without any previous memories."†

Cézanne, in Rilke's view, was able to be fully present to the
present and could therefore see reality as it is. This was also Rilke's
own desire. He suffered from his inability to be fully in the present
and thus see clearly. He writes, "One lives so badly, because one
always comes into the present unfinished, unable, distracted. I
cannot think back on any time of my life without such reproaches
or worse. I believe that the only time I lived without loss were the
ten days after Ruth's [Rilke's daughter] birth, when I found reality
as indescribable, down to its smallest details, as it surely always
is."‡

Cézanne's paintings revealed to Rilke a man able to live

* *Letters on Cézanne,* New York, International Publishing Corporation, 1985,
p. viii.
  † *Ibid.,* p. xv.
  ‡ *Ibid.,* p. 10.

"without loss," totally present to the present, truly seeing. This was Rilke's own search.

I am so glad for this encounter with Rilke and Cézanne because they both bring me closer to the place where true living and true seeing are one.

Right Glory and Vain Glory

(Thursday, December 19)

There are many small "formation groups" at L'Arche. There are groups on peace, on conflict resolution, on medical issues. There are groups on spirituality, politics, and economics. Jean Vanier asked me to lead a group on the Gospel of John. Tonight we had our third meeting.

We spoke about the word "glory." I have gradually become aware how central this word is in John's Gospel. There is God's glory, the right glory that leads to life. And there is human glory, the vain glory that leads to death. All through his Gospel John shows how we are tempted to prefer vain glory over the glory that comes from God.

This idea did not affect me greatly until I realized that human glory is always connected with some form of competition. Human glory is the result of being considered better, faster, more beautiful, more powerful, or more successful than others. Glory conferred by people is glory which results from being favorably compared to other people. The better our scores on the scoreboard of life, the more glory we receive. This glory comes with upward mobility. The higher we climb on the ladder of success, the more glory we collect. But this same glory also creates our darkness. Human glory, based on competition, leads to rivalry; rivalry carries within it the beginning of violence; and violence is the way to death. Thus human glory proves to be vain glory, false glory, mortal glory.

How then do we come to see and receive God's glory? In his Gospel, John shows that God chose to reveal his glory to us in his humiliation. That is the good, but also disturbing, news. God, in his infinite wisdom, chose to reveal his divinity to us not through competition, but through compassion, that is, through suffering with us. God chose the way of downward mobility. Every time Jesus speaks about being glorified and giving glory, he always refers to his humiliation and death. It is through the way of the cross that Jesus gives glory to God, receives glory from God, and makes God's glory known to us. The glory of the resurrection can never be separated from the glory of the cross. The risen Lord always shows us his wounds.

Thus the glory of God stands in contrast to the glory of people. People seek glory by moving upward. God reveals his glory by moving downward. If we truly want to see the glory of God, we must move downward with Jesus. This is the deepest reason for living in solidarity with poor, oppressed, and handicapped people. They are the ones through whom God's glory can manifest itself to us. They show us the way to God, the way to salvation.

This is what L'Arche is beginning to teach me.

Becoming Friends

(Saturday, December 21)

Nathan and I are gradually becoming close friends. It is wonderful to experience the birth of a new friendship. I have always considered friendship to be one of the greatest gifts God has given me. It is the most life-giving gift I can imagine. Since I came to Trosly, I have met many wonderful, loving, and caring people. They have been a source of great joy to me. I know that when I leave we will remember each other with gratitude and fondness but will find it hard to sustain lasting relationships of mutual love and support. It is therefore a beautiful experience to discover that out of the many, someone is emerging who is becoming a friend, a new companion in life, a new presence that will last wherever I will go.

Nathan is a Canadian. His parents, who are Baptists, are the founders of "King's Fold," a small retreat center near Calgary. Two years ago Nathan entered the Catholic Church; soon after that he came to L'Arche in Trosly to live and work with the handicapped. He is a man of deep compassion. When I see him with his friends in the foyer, I am deeply moved by the generous affection he shows to men and women who are so deeply broken. It is the fruit of caring for his own handicapped brother, who died a few years ago.

Over the past few months we have gradually come to know each other. I was not aware of how significant our relationship had become for me until he left for a month to visit his family and friends in Canada. I missed his presence greatly and looked forward to his return.

Two days ago he came back, and tonight we went out for supper together. I felt a need to let him know how much I had missed him. I told him that his absence had made me aware of a real affection for him that had grown in me since we had come to know each other. He responded with a strong affirmation of our friendship from his side. As we talked more about past experiences and future plans, it became clear that God had brought us close for a reason. Nathan hopes to begin theological studies in Toronto in September and plans to live at Daybreak during that time. I am filled with gratitude and joy that God is not only calling me to a new country and a new community, but also offering me a new friendship to make it easier to follow that call.

Listening Together

(Sunday, December 22)

Today the Gospel of the Visitation is read in preparation for Christmas. In recent months the story of Mary's visit to her cousin Elizabeth has become very dear to me.

Mary receives the great and shocking news that she is going to become the Mother of the "Son of the Most High." This news is so incomprehensible and so radically interrupts Mary's humble life that she finds herself totally alone. How can Joseph or any of her friends or relatives understand her situation? With whom can she share this most intimate knowledge, which remains inexplicable even to herself?

God does not want her to be alone with the new life given to her. The angel says, "your cousin Elizabeth also, in her old age, has conceived a son, and she whom people called barren is now in her sixth month, for nothing is impossible to God" (Luke 1:36–37).

God offers Mary an intimate, human friend with whom she can share what seems incommunicable. Elizabeth, like Mary, has experienced divine intervention and has been called to a response of faith. She can be with Mary in a way no one else possibly could.

Thus, it is understandable that "Mary set out at that time and went as quickly as she could into the hill country to a town in Judah" (Luke 1:39) to visit Elizabeth.

I am deeply moved by this simple and mysterious encounter. In the midst of an unbelieving, doubting, pragmatic, and cynical world, two women meet each other and affirm in each other the promise given to them. The humanly impossible has happened to them. God has come to them to begin the salvation promised through the ages. Through these two women God has decided to change the course of history. Who could ever understand? Who could ever believe it? Who could ever let it happen? But Mary says, "Let it happen to me," and she immediately realizes that only Elizabeth will be able to affirm her "yes." For three months Mary and Elizabeth live together and encourage each other to truly accept the motherhood given to them. Mary's presence makes Elizabeth more fully aware of becoming the mother of the "prophet of the Most High" (Luke 1:76), and Elizabeth's presence allows Mary to grow in the knowledge of becoming the mother of the "Son of the Most High" (Luke 1:32).

Neither Mary nor Elizabeth had to wait in isolation. They could wait together and thus deepen in each other their faith in God, for whom nothing is impossible. Thus, God's most radical intervention into history was listened to and received in community.

The story of the Visitation teaches me the meaning of friendship and community. How can I ever let God's grace fully work in my life unless I live in a community of people who can affirm it, deepen it, and strengthen it? We cannot live this new life alone. God does not want to isolate us by his grace. On the contrary, he wants us to form new friendships and a new community—holy places where his grace can grow to fullness and bear fruit.

So often new life appears in the Church because of an encounter. Dorothy Day never claimed *The Catholic Worker* as her own invention. She always spoke of it as the fruit of her encounter with Peter Maurin. Jean Vanier never claims that he started L'Arche on his own. He always points to his encounter with Père Thomas Philippe as the true beginning of L'Arche. In such encounters two or more people are able to affirm each other in their gifts and encourage each other to "let it happen to them." In this way, new hope is given to the world.

Elizabeth helped Mary to become the Mother of God. Mary helped Elizabeth to become the mother of her Son's prophet, John the Baptist. God may choose us individually, but he always wants us to come together to allow his choice to come to maturity.

A Christmas Prayer

(Monday, December 23)

O Lord, how hard it is to accept your way. You come to me as a small, powerless child born away from home. You live for me as a stranger in your own land. You die for me as a criminal outside the walls of the city, rejected by your own people, misunderstood by your friends, and feeling abandoned by your God.

As I prepare to celebrate your birth, I am trying to feel loved, accepted, and at home in this world, and I am trying to overcome the feelings of alienation and separation which continue to assail me. But I wonder now if my deep sense of homelessness does not bring me closer to you than my occasional feelings of belonging. Where do I truly celebrate your birth: in a cozy home or in an unfamiliar house, among welcoming friends or among unknown strangers, with feelings of well-being or with feelings of loneliness?

I do not have to run away from those experiences that are closest to yours. Just as you do not belong to this world, so I do not belong to this world. Every time I feel this way I have an occasion to be grateful and to embrace you better and taste more fully your joy and peace.

Come, Lord Jesus, and be with me where I feel poorest. I trust that this is the place where you will find your manger and bring your light. Come, Lord Jesus, come.

Amen.

Prepare!

(Tuesday, December 24)

Père Thomas keeps telling us in his sermons that the days before Christmas must be days of deep prayer to prepare our hearts for the coming of Christ. We must be really ready to receive him. Christ wants to be born in us, but we must be open, willing, receptive, and truly welcoming. To become that way we have Advent and especially the last days before Christmas.

Often, if not daily, I tell myself, "Today I am going to spend some extra time just praying, just waiting expectantly, just sitting quietly." But always the day seems to be consumed by a thousand little things which beg for my attention. When the day is over I feel frustrated, angry, and disappointed with myself.

Especially today! This morning I thought the day was completely free and open for prayer. Now it is evening, and I don't know where the time went. Somehow the externals of Christmas —presents, decorations, short visits—took over and the day drained away like water through a poorly built dike. How hard it is to remember Père André's words about the difference between the urgent and the important!

I often think, "A life is like a day; it goes by so fast. If I am so careless with my days, how can I be careful with my life?" I know that somehow I have not fully come to believe that urgent things can wait while I attend to what is truly important. It finally boils down to a question of deep and strong conviction. Once I am truly convinced that preparing the heart is more important than preparing the Christmas tree, I will be a lot less frustrated at the end of the day.

I wish I had better things to write on Christmas Eve. But better write what is true than what is pious. God is coming. He comes to a restless, somewhat anxious heart. I offer him my frustration and confusion and trust that he will do something with it.

A "Dry" Christmas

(Wednesday, December 25)

Christmas has arrived again. Night Mass was festive with many green branches, red lights, and white-robed altar boys. The church was packed, the songs sweet, and Père Thomas's sermon moving. The dawn Mass, which I celebrated in English in Madame Vanier's dining room, was simple and quiet. The 11 A.M. day Mass was joyful and rich with many good words from the good Père.

Père Thomas explained that the mystery of Christmas was so deep that the Church needs three Masses to express itself. It is an event that touches our innermost self, our life in family and community, and the whole created order.

There was a big dinner after the day Mass, and we exchanged gifts. In the afternoon I slept a little, talked a little with Madame Vanier and Jo Cork, who had just arrived from the Daybreak community in Canada, and wrote a little.

Everything was there to make a splendid Christmas. But I wasn't really there. I felt like a sympathetic observer. I couldn't force myself to feel differently. It just seemed that I wasn't part of it. At times I even caught myself looking at it all like an unbeliever who wonders what everybody is so busy and excited about. Spiritually, this is a dangerous attitude. It creates a certain sarcasm, cynicism, and depression. But I didn't want or choose it. I just found myself in a mental state that I could not move out of by my own force.

Still, in the midst of it all I saw—even though I did not feel— that this day may prove to be a grace after all. Somehow I realized that songs, music, good feelings, beautiful liturgies, nice presents, big dinners, and many sweet words do not make Christmas.

Christmas is saying "yes" to something beyond all emotions and feelings. Christmas is saying "yes" to a hope based on God's initiative, which has nothing to do with what I think or feel. Christmas is believing that the salvation of the world is God's work and not mine. Things will never look just right or feel just right. If they did, someone would be lying. The world is not whole, and today I experienced this fact in my own unhappiness. But it is into this broken world that a child is born who is called Son of the Most High, Prince of Peace, Savior.

I look at him and pray, "Thank you, Lord, that you came, independent of my feelings and thoughts. Your heart is greater than mine." Maybe a "dry" Christmas, a Christmas without much to feel or think, will bring me closer to the true mystery of God-with-us. What it asks is pure, naked faith.

12

Going Home

Apprehension

(The Netherlands; Thursday, December 26)

After celebrating the Eucharist with Madame Vanier and Jo Cork, Barbara drove me to the railroad station in Compiègne, where I took the train to my home country.

Traveling to my family and friends in Holland fills me with apprehension and a certain fear. Most of those with whom I shared my youth have moved away from the Church and have little connection with anything even vaguely spiritual. Speaking about spiritual things to spiritual people is quite easy. But speaking about God and God's presence in our hearts, our families, and our daily lives to people for whom "God words" are often connected with hurtful memories seems nearly impossible.

So here I am traveling through my own country. I know its language better than any other, but do I have the words to say what I truly want to say? As I go from Rosendaal to Breda to Eindhoven to Helmond, I pray the rosary. The Hail Marys make me aware that I have to be very quiet, very simple, and perhaps very silent.

A Surprising Visitor

(Friday, December 27)

My first day home was good and surprising. Good, because my eighty-two-year-old father welcomed me warmly. He is in good health and good spirits, vitally interested in national and international affairs, and eager to talk about them. Although he had just sold his large judicial library, his reading chair was surrounded with many new books about literature, history, and art. He kept saying, "Have you read this . . . and that . . . and this . . . it is very interesting." It is good to be home, in a house so richly filled with memories of a long and well-lived life.

It was also a surprising day because the mayor of Eindhoven, the city where the Phillips Corporation has its main factories, called to say he wanted to see me. He arrived a few hours later. I had no idea why the mayor of Eindhoven wanted to see me so urgently. I had never heard of him before and did not know that he had heard of me. But he had read one of my books and called my father to ask when I would be home.

Gilles Borrie proved to be a wonderful, warm, and very gentle person who just wanted to speak about the "things of God." It was a heart-to-heart conversation. We spoke about the Church in Holland, about the Trappist life, about prayer, and about our continuing search for God. In the middle of the conversation Gilles's wife called to tell him that his mother had just suffered a stroke and was dying. She was in her nineties but had been very healthy and alert until now. Suddenly our relationship deepened. We became friends in a moment of shock and grief. We prayed together and reflected on this crucial moment of Gilles's life. Then he left with the firm promise to stay in touch.

I was deeply moved that without doing or planning anything, I had been put in touch with a man searching for God and called to accompany him in his grief. It felt as if God wanted to welcome me back to my own country and say, "Don't be too nervous about finding the right language or the right tone, but trust that my spirit will speak through you, even when you are least prepared."

Smart but Distracted

(Saturday, December 28)

The most remarkable thing about Holland is its prosperity. Unlike in France, England, or the United States, there are almost no poor people. Wherever you go people look well fed, well dressed, and well housed. This Christmas especially, it seemed that everyone was able to buy what they wanted, eat what they liked, and go where they wished. Countless Dutch people went to Switzerland or Austria to ski; others stayed home eating, drinking, and watching TV, and a few attended well-prepared and carefully orchestrated worship services. The country feels very self-satisfied. There is not much space left, inside or outside, to be with God and God alone.

It is hard to explain why Holland changed from a very pious to a very secular country in one generation. Many reasons can be given. But it seems to me, from just looking around and meeting and speaking to people, that their captivating prosperity is one of the more obvious reasons. People are just very busy—eating, drinking, and going places.

Paul van Vliet, a well-known Dutch comedian, used, as one of the themes in his Christmas TV show, "We are smart but very distracted." Indeed, we know and understand what we most need, but we just don't get around to it, since we are so busy playing with our toys. There is too much to play with! No real time to grow up and do the necessary thing: "Love God and each other."

The Dutch have become a distracted people—very good, kind, and good-natured but caught in too much of everything.

Asking to Be Sent

(Monday, December 30)

At 10 A.M. I met with my bishop, Cardinal Simonis of Utrecht. I explained to him the call from the Daybreak community and asked if he would be willing to send me there.

It has become increasingly important for me to go where I am not only called, but also sent. Being called to live and work in Canada seems to be a good thing, but if it is not supported by a mission from the Church, I don't think it will bear much fruit.

Knowing that the place where you live and the work you do is not simply your own choice but part of a mission makes all the difference. When difficulties arise, the knowledge of being sent will give me the strength not to run away, but to be faithful. When the work proves tiring, the facilities poor, and the relationships frustrating, I can say, "These hardships are not a reason to leave, but an occasion to purify my heart."

Cardinal Simonis asked me if I felt that being called there was a response to my own prayers. I could honestly say "yes" to that. Often I have prayed, "Lord, show me the way and I will follow you." Jean Vanier's invitation to introduce me to L'Arche and the call from Daybreak that grew from that first invitation were a clear response to that prayer. Yet because I am a priest ordained to serve my bishop, the affirmation of the Church is of crucial importance. To feel called is not enough. It is necessary to be sent.

At the end of our conversation the bishop said, "My first response is that I think you should go there, but give me a few days and call me Saturday at noon. That will give me a chance to read the letter you received from Daybreak and to think a little more about it."

It was a good conversation. Compared to my conversations with Jean Vanier, Père Thomas, and Père André, it was more distant and pragmatic—questions about financial responsibility, pension, and insurance came up quite soon—but I am not in France, but in Holland, asking not for spiritual guidance or emotional support, but for a new mandate. Cardinal Simonis is my bishop, who for me represents the authority of the Church. If he affirms my call, I hope that he will not only give me permission, but truly send me to this new ministry.

A Lonely New Year's Eve

(Tuesday, December 31)

Somehow this has been a hard day for me. Early this morning I walked around Utrecht trying to find a church where I could go to pray. But the two churches I came upon were closed, and when I rang the rectory doorbell, there was no response. As I walked through the streets saying the rosary, I felt like a stranger among my own people.

Later I took a train to Amsterdam to visit a friend, and from there I went to Rotterdam to celebrate New Year's Eve with my brother and his family. At 7 P.M. I celebrated the Eucharist in the nearby parish church. My little six-year-old niece was willing to go with me, but everyone else preferred to stay home. Except for the sacristan, little Sarah, and myself, there was nobody in the big old church. I felt lonely, especially because I couldn't share God's gifts with those who are closest to me. My deepest thoughts and feelings have become foreign to them.

The event that followed was pleasant and friendly, with a splendid dinner, good easy conversation, and champagne to welcome the New Year. No prayers or scripture readings as in the past. I keep wondering how, in one generation, such a pious family could lose so completely its connection with God and God's church. It is hard for me to celebrate with my whole being when there is so little to celebrate. I feel lonely while being so close to those who are dear to me.

Three Generations

(Wednesday, January 1, 1986)

It has become a sort of tradition that I celebrate the Eucharist on the first day of the year with the Van Campen family in Lieshout, near Eindhoven. The Van Campens have been friends of my parents as long as I can remember. In October 1978, the same month that my mother died, Phillip Van Campen, sixty-eight, had a severe stroke. He has been paralyzed ever since. Once a successful bank director and businessman, he has now become an invalid totally dependent on his wife and the nurses who care for him. On his birthday, the first of January, his wife invites their six children and their families to the family home for a Eucharist and a dinner.

For me it is an annual confrontation with the tragedy of Dutch Catholicism. Phillip and his wife, Puck, are both deeply believing people. Their life centers around the Eucharist. Puck, whose days are fully dedicated to the care of her invalid husband, continues to find hope and strength in Jesus through his presence in her life. But for the children the words "God" and "Church" have become much more ambiguous and often evoke very critical and sometimes even hostile thoughts. The two older sons and their families still visit the church regularly. They see the life in Christ as important but often wonder if the services they attend really nurture their spiritual life. The younger children, however, have become much more alienated. For them, the Church has become irrelevant. For most of them the Bible is no longer used, the sacraments have become unknown, prayer is nonexistent, and thoughts about a greater life than the present are rather utopian.

The grandchildren seem most ill at ease with religious ceremonies. Six of them have not been baptized and look at me, vested in alb and stole, as at some performer who is not very entertaining.

It was quite an experience to pray and celebrate the Eucharist surrounded by a large family in which the parents are deeply committed Christians, the children find themselves less and less at home in the Church, and most of the grandchildren have become unfamiliar with the story of God's love.

All of these men and women are very good, caring, and responsible people. Their friendship means a lot to me and gives me joy. Still, I experience a real sadness that the faith that gives so much life to the parents no longer shapes the lives of all the children and grandchildren.

Who is to blame? I often wonder where I would be today if I had been part of the great turmoil of the Dutch Church during the last decades. Blaming is not the issue. What is important is to find the anger-free parts in people's hearts where God's love can be heard and received.

After the Gospel reading I spoke about God's "first love," which allows us to forgive each other for not being able to give one another all the love we desire. I realized that those who had struggled with relationships (and who among us had not?) were listening and making connections. They said "yes" to the pain I described, but not everyone seemed ready yet to say "yes" to the one who came to heal that pain. I wonder if those who are between thirty and fifty and who no longer find the Church a source of strength will ever be able to let Jesus heal their wounds. But maybe one day their children will ask them the old question again: "Is Jesus the Messiah, or do we have to wait for another?"

In Search of Meaning

(Thursday, January 2)

I spent most of the afternoon with one of my best Dutch friends and his family. We first met in the early sixties, when we were working as clinical psychologists in the Dutch army. He now teaches medical psychology at the University of Utrecht and has become a well-known authority on mental health issues. We have stayed in touch, and over the years our friendship has deepened, though we see each other only once a year.

Our discussion soon became quite intimate. We spoke about the existential loneliness we are both experiencing at this time in our lives. This loneliness stems not from a lack of friends, problems with spouse or children, or absence of professional recognition. Neither of us has any major complaints in these areas. Still . . . the question "What am I doing, and for what reason?" lurks underneath all of our good feelings about friends, family, and work. Wim spoke about experiences of "de-realization" which are "beyond psychological explanation." As we have both passed fifty, we have discovered that at times we look at our world with a strange inner question: "What am I doing here? Is this really our world, our people, our existence? What is everybody so busy with?"

This question comes from a place deeper than emotions, feelings, or passions. It is the question about the meaning of existence, raised not just by the mind, but also by a searching heart, a question which makes us feel like strangers in our own milieu. People take on a robotlike quality. They do many things but don't seem to have an interior life. Some outside power seems to "wind them up" and make them do whatever they are doing. This "de-realization" experience is extremely painful, but it can also be the way to a deeper connection.

Wim and I spoke about this deeper connection. Without a

deep-rooted sense of belonging, all of life can easily become cold, distant, and painfully repetitive. This deeper connection is the connection with the one whose name is love, leading to a new discovery that we are born out of love and are always called back to that love. It leads to a new realization that God is the God of life who continues to offer us life wherever and whenever death threatens. It ultimately leads to prayer. And from our being human, being child, brother or sister, father or mother, grandfather or grandmother comes a new experience of being held within the hand of a loving God.

Words Heard but Not Received

(Saturday, January 4)

Today my father celebrated his eighty-third birthday. He had invited all his children and his brothers and sisters, with their spouses, to be with him. We came from all over the country, twenty-one people altogether. At 12:30 P.M. we all went to the village church for the Eucharist.

I had put chairs in the sanctuary so that we could all gather around the altar. Although most of the family were still "practicing Catholics," I felt some distance. I spoke about Jesus, who accompanies us on our lifelong road and explains to us that our struggles and pain can become ways to break through depression and bitterness and discover a deep healing presence. My words were heard, but not received. After the service the only remarks were about cold feet and a slippery road home. One of my uncles said, "Well, you are obviously convinced of what you said. But I do not think that way."

I had hoped to offer a hopeful, life-giving message, but somehow I had not found the words. My brother gave a very funny and sympathetic toast before dinner, using an astrology book to describe my father's character. His words were eagerly received and much applauded. He knew his audience much better than I did.

The feeling of having become something of a stranger in my own family was strong throughout the whole day. I had not seen many of the people at the party for more than a decade. Our reunion made me realize how much had happened to them and to me, and made me sadly aware that I no longer know the soil on which we both stand.

My father, meanwhile, was strong, happy, and exuberant. For him the main question is how to stay young, while for me it is how to grow old. My concern about being prepared for the great encounter with the Lord was not shared.

In the midst of it all, I called Cardinal Simonis to ask his final word about going to Daybreak. He said, "Do it." He had talked about it with his staff and come to the conclusion that it was a good idea. But he also said, "Do it for three years, and maybe then you might be interested in returning to your motherland. It seems good to keep that option open."

I was very glad to have the Cardinal's blessing on my future. I mentioned it excitedly to my father and the rest of the family. But their minds were elsewhere. What for me was a major turning point in my life was for them another item of news among people trying to catch up with each other. It may be small news, but it is good news for me.

13

The Struggle of Prayer

The Way to Pray

(Trosly, France; Friday, January 10)

Prayer continues to be very difficult. Still, every morning when I walk in the garden of La Ferme saying the rosary and spending an hour in the oratory simply being in God's presence, I know that I am not wasting my time. Though I am terribly distracted, I know that God's spirit is at work in me. Though I have no deeply religious insights or feelings, I am aware of the peace beyond thoughts and emotions. Though my early-morning prayer seems quite unsuccessful, I always look forward to it and guard it as a special time.

A short piece on prayer by Dom John Chapman published in the December 14th *Tablet* has given me much hope. It is taken from one of his spiritual letters. He writes:

> Prayer, in the sense of union with God, is the most crucifying thing there is. One must do it for God's sake; but one will not get any satisfaction out of it, in the sense of feeling "I am good at prayer. I have an infallible method." That would be disastrous, since what we want to learn is precisely our

own weakness, powerlessness, unworthiness. Nor ought one to expect "a sense of the reality of the supernatural" of which I speak. And one should wish for no prayer, except precisely the prayer that God gives us—probably very distracted and unsatisfactory in every way.

On the other hand, the only way to pray is to pray; and the way to pray well is to pray much. If one has no time for this, then one must at least pray regularly. But the less one prays, the worse it goes. And if circumstances do not permit even regularity, then one must put up with the fact that when one does try to pray, one can't pray—and our prayer will probably consist of telling this to God.

As to beginning afresh, or where you left off, I don't think you have any choice. You simply have to begin wherever you find yourself. Make any acts you want to make and feel you ought to make, but do not force yourself into *feelings* of any kind.

You say very naturally that you do not know what to do if you have a quarter of an hour alone in church. Yes, I suspect the only thing to do is to shut out the church and everything else, and just give yourself to God and beg him to have mercy on you, and offer him all your distractions.*

The sentence that I like most is, ". . . the only way to pray is to pray; and the way to pray well is to pray much." Chapman's sound wisdom really helps me. No-nonsense advice, and very true. It all boils down to his main point: We must pray not first of all because it feels good or helps, but because God loves us and wants our attention.

* *The Spiritual Letters of Dom John Chapman, O.S.B.*, London: Sheed and Ward, 1938, pp. 52–53. Quoted in *The Tablet*, December 14, 1985.

Choosing the Way of Humility

(Sunday, January 12)

Today is the feast of the baptism of the Lord. I have been thinking much about this feast, yesterday and today. Jesus, who is without sin, stands in line with sinners waiting to be baptized by John. As Jesus starts his ministry, he chooses to enter into solidarity with sinful humanity. "John tried to dissuade him with the words 'It is I who need baptism from you, and yet you come to me.' But Jesus replied, 'Leave it like this for the time being; it is fitting that we should, in this way, do all that uprightness demands' " (Matthew 3:14–15).

Here we see how Jesus clearly chooses the way of humility. He does not appear with great fanfare as a powerful savior, announcing a new order. On the contrary, he comes quietly, with the many sinners who are receiving a baptism of repentance. His choice is affirmed by the voice from heaven: "This is my Son, the Beloved; my favor rests on him" (Matthew 3:17).

How radical this choice is becomes clear in the temptations that follow. The devil suggests another option: "Be relevant, do something spectacular, accept world power." This is the way of the world. Jesus rejects this option and chooses God's way, a way of humility revealing itself gradually to be the way of the cross.

It is hard to believe that God would reveal his divine presence to us in the self-emptying, humble way of the man from Nazareth. So much in me seeks influence, power, success, and popularity. But the way of Jesus is the way of hiddenness, powerlessness, and littleness. It does not seem a very appealing way. Yet when I enter into true, deep communion with Jesus I will find that it is this small way that leads to real peace and joy.

At this feast of the Lord's baptism, I pray for the courage to choose the small way and to keep choosing it. L'Arche will certainly help me in this.

Healing Prayer

(Tuesday, January 14)

In the first reading of today's liturgy we heard the story of Hannah's prayer in the book of Samuel. Hannah was deeply depressed because Yahweh had made her barren. As she went to the temple she fervently prayed that Yahweh would give her a son and thus take her humiliation away. Her prayer was so intense that the priest, Eli, thought she was drunk. But she said to him, "No, my Lord, I am a woman in great trouble; I have not been drinking wine or strong drink—I am pouring out my soul before Yahweh. Do not take your servant for a worthless woman; all this time I have been speaking from the depth of my grief and resentment" (1 Samuel 1:15–16).

Eli then blessed her, and when she came home her depression left her and "she began eating and was dejected no longer" (1 Samuel 1:18). Later she conceived and gave birth to a son whom she called Samuel.

What touches me most in this story is that depression left Hannah after her prayer, but long before Yahweh responded to it by giving her a son. It was her agonizing prayer, which brought all of her feelings of humiliation, rejection, and resentment before God, that took her inner darkness away. Her husband, Elkanah, had not been able to console her, even though he had said to her, "Hannah, why are you crying? Why are you not eating anything? Why are you so sad? Am I not more to you than ten sons?" (1 Samuel 1:8). But when she had poured out all "the bitterness of her soul" (1 Samuel 1:10) to God and had allowed God to touch her, she became a new woman and knew that God would hear her prayer.

Prayer heals. Not just the answer to prayer. When we give up our competition with God and offer God every part of our heart, holding back nothing at all, we come to know God's love for us and discover how safe we are in his embrace. Once we know again that God has not rejected us, but keeps us close to his heart, we can find again the joy of living, even though God might guide our life in a different direction from our desires.

Prayer is so important. It invites us to live in ever closer communion with the one who loves us more than any human being ever can. After her prayer, Hannah knew once again that she was loved by God. In prayer she rediscovered her true self. Her happiness was no longer dependent upon having a child, but only upon the total and unlimited love of God. Thus she could wipe away her tears, eat again, and see her depression depart. When God in his love gave her a son, she was truly grateful. Because God's goodness, not her own, was the main source of her joy.

A Prayer of Abandonment

(Wednesday, January 15)

This morning during my hour of prayer, I tried to come to some level of abandonment to my heavenly Father. It was a hard struggle since so much in me wants to do my will, realize my plans, organize my future, and make my decisions. Still, I know that true joy comes from letting God love me the way God wants, whether it is through illness or health, failure or success, poverty or wealth, rejection or praise. It is hard for me to say, "I shall gratefully accept everything, Lord, that pleases you. Let your will be done." But I know that when I truly believe my Father is pure love, it will become increasingly possible to say these words from the heart.

Charles de Foucauld once wrote a prayer of abandonment that expresses beautifully the spiritual attitude I wish I had. Sometimes I pray it, even though the words do not yet fully come from my heart. I will write them down here:

> Father,
> I abandon myself into your hands;
> do with me what you will.
> Whatever you may do, I thank you;
> I am ready for all, I accept all.
> Let only your will be done in me,
> and in all your creatures.
>
> I wish no more than this,
> O Lord.
>
> Into your hands I commend my soul;
> I offer it to you with all the love
> of my heart,
> for I love you, Lord,
> and so need to give myself,
> to surrender myself into your hands,
> without reserve
> and with boundless confidence.
> For you are my Father.

It seems good to pray this prayer often. These are the words of a holy man, and they show the way I must go. I realize that I can never make this prayer come true by my own efforts. But the spirit of Jesus given to me can help me pray it and grow to its fulfillment. I know that my inner peace depends on my willingness to make this prayer my own.

14

Deep Roots

An Invitation

(Thursday, January 16)

On Sunday, January 19, Mr. Herman Herder, president of the Herder Publishing Company, will celebrate his sixtieth birthday. I have been invited to participate in the celebration. So tomorrow I will go to Freiburg in Germany. There will be a dinner, an organ concert, a reception, and a lecture by Rudolf Schnackenburg. I look forward to being part of it all.

I have decided to use this occasion to stay for six weeks in Germany to work closely with my German editor and to finish a small book on icons.

Beauty and Order

(Freiburg, West Germany; Friday, January 17)

Another language, another style, another "tone." I continue to be surprised by how small Europe is and how great the differences are between people who live so close to each other.

I took the train from Paris to Strasbourg. There Franz Johna, my friend and editor at Verlag Herder, met me and drove me over the border to Freiburg. A beautiful, charming, rather intimate city built around the splendid Münster Cathedral, Freiburg sits like a precious gem in the valley between the Rhine and the first hills of the Black Forest. It is a university town, with very little industry. The center is kept free from cars. People walk in the middle of the streets, which are lined by narrow gutters of running water. There are many beautiful churches, city gates, small medieval-looking alleys, and little squares with contemporary sculptures. It is a new city completely rebuilt after the Second World War. Yet it is a very old city rebuilt in the style and atmosphere of ages past. Everyone looks well-to-do. The stores are many and filled with a great variety of goods: clothes, food, books, modern appliances, artwork, and so on. There seems to be no end to the abundance.

At 11 P.M. Franz drove me to my place of residence, the mother house of the Vincentian Sisters in the Habsburger Strasse. The sisters received me with enthusiasm and warm hospitality and gave me a large room to stay in. I feel very happy to be here. I have been in this country only a few times in my life and always for a very short time. The occupation of Holland during the Second World War made it hard for us to go to Germany. Somehow all my attention was directed westward. But now I can get to know a new country, a new people, and a new way of praising God.

The Deeper Question

(Tuesday, January 21)

My breakfast and dinner discussions with the priests who live in the mother house of the Vincentian Sisters have helped me to get some idea of the struggles of the Church in Germany. That these struggles are not minor became clear from the simple fact that my fellow priests disagreed with each other on most issues they discussed. I was often the surprised witness of fierce debates involving both body and mind.

Still, there is agreement about one thing. Questions concerning birth control, abortion, and euthanasia, as well as questions about the Pope, bishops' appointments, clerical dress, liturgical styles, and so on, are all symptoms of a much deeper question, which is, "Do we truly believe in God?" The Germans, no less than the French and the Dutch, have moved into a new age. The existence of God, the divinity of Christ, and the spiritual authority of the Church are no longer foundational elements of Western European society. Whereas the society of the seventeenth, eighteenth, and nineteenth centuries could still build upon a value system deeply molded by the Christian tradition, the late twentieth century finds hardly a common value left. When it comes to legislation about central social issues such as giving life and causing death, there is no longer a common point of reference considered sacred by all. The central Christian vision, that life is a gift from God, to be nurtured, developed, and at all cost respected, no longer guides the decisions of all lawmakers. Thus laws, rules, and regulations tend to become increasingly functional and pragmatic. The question then becomes, "What seems best at present for the majority of the people?"

Meanwhile, many church leaders spend and often waste precious energy on issues which do more to distract us than to deepen our sense of mission. Progressives and conservatives fight each other within the Church, but both are in constant danger of becoming completely irrelevant to what molds our contemporary society.

Is there a God who cares? Are there any signs that history is guided by a merciful hand? Are there relationships which reach beyond the limits of the interpersonal, intercommunal, or international? Is life more than what psychologists, sociologists, biologists, and chemists can define? Is there anything to hope for after we have returned to dust? These questions are far from speculative. They touch the core of our civilization. Is the Church prepared to deal with these issues not just on an intellectual level, but on the level of daily life? Many Germans who still go to church no longer believe in a life after death. They come for very different reasons than the words they read or hear in church suggest. It is doubtful that they will stay very long.

The coming weeks will give me ample chance to think about all of this. I am happy to have fellow priests to help me articulate the questions and think about them. It forces me to go to the heart of the Christian faith, first of all my own.

Predictability: Virtue and Liability

(Wednesday, January 22)

Living in a country in which little or no place remains for the unexpected or the surprising, the reading about David's election by Samuel and his victory over Goliath offers a real warning to me. I must confess that I like the predictability of life as it is lived here. When people tell me that they will pick me up at 4 P.M., they do not come a minute earlier or later. When the concert is supposed to start at 5 P.M., the first organ tones can be heard a moment after the clock has sounded its five strokes. When they tell me that the meal will be served at 6:15 P.M., it *is* served at 6:15 P.M. And the places are as proper as the times are precise. Everything has its place. Returning to my room after breakfast, I find everything back in the place where it was before I touched it.

For the time being, this great predictability offers me much peace. The absence of the unexpected allows me to work steadily on the realization of my plans. But still, David was the least expected king and his victory over Goliath the least predictable outcome of the battle with the Philistines. And what about Jesus, the "son of David"? Of him Nathanael says, "What good can come from Nazareth?" (John 1:46). And many of Jesus' followers lived lives as surprising as that of their master. There is a way of organizing life that leaves no room for the unpredictable. Maybe that explains that while many young German men and women have spent long periods of time at L'Arche in France, they have not yet been able to build L'Arche communities in Germany itself. Care for the handicapped in Germany is so well organized that the rather casual, somewhat free-floating style of L'Arche finds little acceptance. But can the spirit of God be bound? Jesus says, "The wind blows where it pleases . . . so it is with everyone who is born of the Spirit" (John 3:8). And Paul writes, "Do not stifle the Spirit" (1 Thessalonians 5:19).

If I want to get my work done, Germany is probably the best place to be. But if I want to give the spirit a real chance to work in me, I had better keep some of the French "laissez-faire" alive within me.

Proclaiming
the Riches of Christ

(Friday, January 24)

Today, my fifty-fourth birthday, the text of the first reading of the liturgy in honor of St. Francis de Sales summarizes my feelings succinctly. Paul writes to the Ephesians: "I, who am less than the least of all God's holy people, have been entrusted with this special grace, of proclaiming to the Gentiles the unfathomable treasure of Christ and of throwing light on the inner workings of the mystery kept hidden through all the ages in God, the Creator of everything" (Ephesians 3:8–9).

As I reflect on my life today, I feel indeed like the least of God's holy people. Looking back, I realize that I am still struggling with the same problems I had on the day of my ordination twenty-nine years ago. Notwithstanding my many prayers, my periods of retreat, and the advice from many friends, counselors, and confessors, very little, if anything, has changed with regard to my search for inner unity and peace. I am still the restless, nervous, intense, distracted, and impulse-driven person I was when I set out on this spiritual journey. At times this obvious lack of inner maturation depresses me as I enter into the "mature" years.

But I have one source of consolation. More than ever I feel the desire to proclaim "the unfathomable riches of Christ" and to throw light "on the inner working of the mystery kept hidden through all the ages in God." This desire has grown in intensity and urgency. I want to speak about the riches of Christ much more than when I was ordained in 1957. I vividly remember that the man who ordained me, Bernard Cardinal Alfrink, had written, on his coat of arms, "Evangelizare Divitias Christi" ("to proclaim the riches of Christ"). Today, when I read these same words in the liturgy, I realize that I have made these words increasingly my own. I really do want to speak loudly and clearly about the great riches of Christ. I want to do it simply, directly, plainly, and with deep personal conviction. Here I feel that something has grown in me. Here I sense that I am not the same person that I was twenty-nine years ago.

Maybe an increasing awareness of my sinfulness, as well as an increasing desire to make known the unfathomable riches of Christ, will prevent me from becoming proud, self-righteous, manipulative, and oppressive. I pray today that my sins will make me humble and my call to witness for Christ courageous. Francis de Sales is the best possible example I can have on this day to thank

God for my life and to ask for faithfulness to the ministry given to me.

A Medieval Lesson in Humility

(Monday, January 27)

One of the stone reliefs of the Romanesque portal of the Münster, the splendid cathedral of Freiburg dating from about 1210, attempts to nudge the churchgoer in a playful way toward humility. A king is seated in a small basket which is hanging by a cord bound on both ends to the necks of two huge birds. The king holds in his hands two long spits on which two rabbits are impaled. By trying to reach the rabbits with their beaks, the hungry birds lift up the king into the air.

This comic relief portrays the story of Alexander the Great, who, after having conquered the whole world, also tries to make it to heaven. Although different versions of the story exist, one of them says that when Alexander saw the earth beneath him as a small hat in a large sea, he realized how tiny the world really is and how ridiculous it had been to spend his life trying to conquer it. Thus Alexander is presented to the pious churchgoer as an example of silly pride.

Konrad Kunze, the author of the beautiful book about the Münster entitled *Heaven in Stone*, summarizes a sermon of Berthold von Regensburg given around 1260: "Alexander, for whom the world was too small, becomes in the end only seven feet of dust, just like the poorest man ever born; Alexander thought that he could pull down the highest stars from heaven with his hands. And you, as he, would love to go up in the air, if you could only do it. But the story of Alexander shows the result of such high flying, and proves that the great Alexander was one of the greatest fools the world has ever seen."*

Well, no subtleties here! I wonder what Berthold would have thought about Boeing 747s. Still . . . the Münster itself, with its high-rising Gothic arches, might prove to be as much a sign of civic pride as of humility in the eyes of God. People always had mixed motives! God have mercy on us.

Human Grief

(Thursday, January 30)

All the newspapers are proclaiming the tragic death of seven astronauts. The United States grieves. Millions who saw it happen on TV are still in shock, most of all the children who came to see one of their teachers participate in the great adventure of space exploration. They expected to see human greatness, and they saw human vulnerability.

Many people worry about the lasting effects of this tragedy on the children who saw it happen before their eyes. In the United States death has become almost invisible. Suddenly it becomes so visible that its significance can hardly be grasped. How can we grieve and help others to grieve? Do we grieve about a failure in our human ability to conquer space? Do we grieve about the deaths of our heroes, who risked their lives in the service of human progress? Do we grieve in order to find new energy to continue the work begun with so much self-assurance?

When I think about the fact that the United States space program is closely tied to the defense program and that this tragedy is at least in part the result of an international race for superiority and world domination, I cannot but wonder if the grief will lead to peace or to a more determined preparation for war. After

* Konrad Kunze, *Himmel in Stein: Das Freiburger Münster,* Freiburg: Herder, 1980, pp. 84–85.

all, the Strategic Defense Initiative is being prepared for in part by the space shuttle program.

Real human grief means allowing the illusion of immortality to die in us. When those whom we love with an "endless love" die, something also has to die within us. If we do not allow this to happen, we will lose touch with reality, our lives will become increasingly artificial, and we will lose our human capacity for compassion.

The national grief for the death of the seven astronauts will be fruitful if it helps us to die to our vainglory and our national desire to be the best and the most powerful at all costs, and stimulates us to search for a way of peace not dependent on military superiority. Christa McAuliffe stepped into the *Challenger* in the hope of teaching her children something new about the universe in which they live. The real challenge now will be to help these children understand and accept without fear the brokenness and mortality of their parents, their teachers, their heroes, and themselves. If this tragedy gradually helps them to love themselves and the adults who guide them as precious, extremely vulnerable, mortal human beings, they may become peacemakers for whom solidarity and compassion are greater gifts than technical genius and the ability to dominate others.

A Stern Guide

(Tuesday, February 4)

This afternoon I went downtown to pay another visit to the Münster. Together with a middle-aged woman, I took a guided tour. It was a wonderful experience. The guide, a retired civil servant, not only told us the history of the church, the names of the architects and artists, and the meaning of the statues, paintings, and altars, he also viewed the tour as an occasion to preach. He saw it as his task to convert us and bring us to prayer.

As he showed us the majestic portal on which both the saved and the condemned are vividly portrayed, he said, "Let us pray that we end up in the right group." As he showed us a large tapestry of Melchizedek, he recounted elaborately the Old Testament story and its eucharistic application. As he explained the New Testament scenes portrayed in stone or glass or on canvas, he quoted long passages from the Gospels by heart. In between the art treasures he demonstrated to us the ugly wooden contemporary confessionals with lights to indicate if they are free or occupied, and exhorted us to go to confession at least once every two weeks.

At times he expressed his political preferences. In the two "emperor chapels" with splendid stained glass windows portraying the powerful Habsburgers, Maximilian I, Phillip I, Charles V, and Ferdinand I, he said, "Today they don't teach schoolchildren about these great men. Now they teach them about Marx and Lenin. But we had better keep thinking about these Christians."

As we walked through the huge central nave, our guide spotted a young man with a cap on his head. The guide told him without subtlety that this was God's house and that he had to remove his cap or leave. The man left, rather perplexed about the encounter. I was shocked by this confronting, pious, nationalistic, and very moralistic guide. It struck me that the man fits the Münster perfectly. His way of guiding reveals both its greatness and its medieval, clerical, and authoritarian qualities. But what about the young man who was sent away? Would he ever be able to come back and discover the gentle all-forgiving love of God?

I bought a few booklets from the guide and promised him I would return. He brings me closer to the mentality of those who built this house of God, which took more than three centuries to finish. He also makes me ask some painful questions about ministry to those who can no longer relate to the powerful God of the Middle Ages but are searching for a tender, compassionate God, who can heal their wounded hearts.

15

Choosing Life

A Plea for the Reflective Mind

(Wednesday, February 5)

Freiburg is the city of Martin Heidegger (1889–1976). Shortly after I arrived here, Franz Johna drove me past 47 Rötebuckweg, where Heidegger lived and wrote many of his philosophical works.

There are few philosophers who have had as much influence on my thinking as Martin Heidegger. Though I never studied Heidegger directly, many of the philosophers, psychologists, and theologians who formed my thinking were deeply influenced by him. Walgrave, Binswanger, and Rahner cannot be fully understood apart from Heidegger's existentialism.

Today I read a short address given in 1955 in Messkirch, his birthplace, in honor of the musician Conrad Kreutzer, who was also born there. The address is entitled "Gelassenheit."

Heidegger states that the greatest danger of our time is that the calculating way of thinking that is part of the technical revolution will become the dominating and exclusive way of thinking.

Why is this so dangerous? Heidegger says, "Because then we would find, together with the highest and the most successful development of our thinking on the calculating level, an indifference toward reflection and a complete thoughtlessness . . . then humanity would have renounced and thrown away what is most its own, its ability to reflect. What is at stake is to save the essence of humanity. What is at stake is to keep alive our reflective thinking *(das Nachdenken)."*

Heidegger calls for an attitude in which we say "yes" to the new techniques, insofar as they serve our daily lives, and "no" when they claim our whole being. He calls for a *Gelassenheit zu Dingen* (letting reality speak) and an openness to the mystery of things. This calmness and openness, Heidegger says, will give us a new rootedness, a new groundedness, a new sense of belonging. Thus we can remain reflective human beings and prevent ourselves from becoming victims of a "calculating" existence.

It is clear how important Heidegger's thoughts remain today. We need to safeguard our reflective minds more than ever. Indirectly, Heidegger also touches on the need for a new spirituality, a new way of being in the world without being of it.

Feeling Protected

(Friday, February 7)

Gradually I am becoming aware of a new dimension in my prayer life. It is hard to find words for it, but it feels like a protective presence of God, Mary, the angels, and the saints that exists in the midst of distractions, fears, temptations, and inner confusion.

While my prayers were not at all intensive or profound, I had a real desire to spend time in prayer this week. I enjoyed just sitting in the small dark side chapel of the mother house of the

* "Gelassenheit," Verlag Günther Neske, Pfüllingen, 1959, p. 25.

Vincentian Sisters. I felt surrounded by goodness, gentleness, kindness, and acceptance. I felt as if angels' wings were keeping me safe: a protective cloud covering me and keeping me there. Though it is very hard to express, this new experience is the experience of being protected against the dangers of a seductive world. But this protection is very soft, gentle, caring. Not the protection of a wall or a metal screen. It is more like a hand on my shoulder or a kiss on my forehead. But for all this protection, I am not taken away from the dangers. I am not lifted from the seductive world. I am not removed from violence, hatred, lust, and greed. In fact, I feel them in the center of my being, screaming for my full attention. They are restless and noisy. Still, this hand, these lips, these eyes are present and I know that I am safe, held in love, cared for, and protected by the good spirits of heaven.

So I am praying while not knowing how to pray. I am resting while feeling restless, at peace while tempted, safe while still anxious, surrounded by a cloud of light while still in darkness, in love while still doubting.

It is such a grace that I have the time to step out of my room any time during the day and go to the chapel just to be there and to be reassured. The angels of God are always waiting there for me and eager to stand around me and cover me with their wings and let me rest, not giving much attention to all that clamors in my inner darkness. They do not say much; they do not explain much. They are just there to let me know that God's heart is so infinitely greater than my own.

The Compassionate
Eyes of Christ

(Saturday, February 8)

Christ on a Donkey, in the Augustiner Museum in Freiburg, is one of the most moving Christ figures I know. I have sent many postcards of it to my friends, and I keep one in my prayer book.

This afternoon I went to the museum to spend some quiet time with this *Christus auf Palmesel* (Christ on palm-donkey). This fourteenth-century sculpture originally comes from Nieder-rotweil, a small town close to Breisach on the Rhine. It was made to be pulled on a cart in the Palm Sunday procession. In 1900 it was sold to the Augustiner Museum, where it now stands in the center of the first exposition hall.

Christ's long, slender face with a high forehead, inward-looking eyes, long hair, and a small forked beard expresses the mystery of his suffering in a way that holds me spellbound. As he rides into Jerusalem surrounded by people shouting "hosanna," "cutting branches from the trees and spreading them in his path" (Matthew 21:8), Jesus appears completely concentrated on something else. He does not look at the excited crowd. He does not wave. He sees beyond all the noise and movement to what is ahead of him: an agonizing journey of betrayal, torture, crucifixion, and death. His unfocused eyes see what nobody around him can see; his high forehead reflects a knowledge of things to come far beyond anyone's understanding.

There is melancholy, but also peaceful acceptance. There is insight into the fickleness of the human heart, but also immense compassion. There is a deep awareness of the unspeakable pain to be suffered, but also a strong determination to do God's will. Above all, there is love, an endless, deep, and far-reaching love born from an unbreakable intimacy with God and reaching out to all people, wherever they are, were, or will be. There is nothing that he does not fully know. There is nobody whom he does not fully love.

Every time I look at this Christ on the donkey, I am reminded again that I am seen by him with all my sins, guilt, and shame and loved with all his forgiveness, mercy, and compassion.

Just being with him in the Augustiner Museum is a prayer. I look and look and look, and I know that he sees the depths of my heart; I do not have to be afraid.

Window Faces

(Monday, February 10)

Rosenmontag (Carnival's Monday) in Freiburg. At 2 P.M. I went
downtown for the carnival parade and saw clowns, bands, small
and large floats, an endless variety of masks, and an abundance of
confetti. It was bitterly cold. People kept themselves warm with
waffles and *Gluhwein* (hot spiced wine). The parade numbered
149 shows, and it took two hours to pass.

Most impressive were the huge masks. They were often
pieces of art expressing a variety of emotions: anger, joy, hatred,
love, goodness, and evil. Some masks were so realistic I could
hardly imagine that the people wearing them had a different
feeling from what the mask expressed.

Some heads were so huge that their wearers' faces could be
seen only through windows in the neck. Many blew trumpets,
flutes, or horns through the windows. I was struck by the contrast
between the faces on the masks and the faces in the windows. The
"window faces" all looked quite serious, compared to the wild
faces on the heads above them. While the parade invited us to be
fools for a day, it convinced me how hard it is for people to relax
and truly celebrate. Also, the people on the sidewalks watching
the parade took it all in with great seriousness. If there had not
been so many bands, it would have been an extremely dull event.
It all had a somewhat obligatory quality. Even wildly dressed
people had a hard time smiling! It was a serious job for them. The
children seemed the most serious of all. Whether they looked like
cats, mice, polar bears, screwdrivers, Indians, Mexicans, or
witches, their little faces showed that they were performing an
important task!

I watched all this, ate a waffle, drank two cups of *Gluhwein*,
and went home. The sister who opened the door greeted me with

an open face, a big smile, and a free laugh. I suddenly realized that no mask can make people really happy. Happiness must come from within.

A Lenten Prayer

(Tuesday, February 11)

Dear Lord Jesus,

Tomorrow the Lenten season begins. It is a time to be with you in a special way, a time to pray, to fast, and thus to follow you on your way to Jerusalem, to Golgotha, and to the final victory over death.

I am still so divided. I truly want to follow you, but I also want to follow my own desires and lend an ear to the voices that speak about prestige, success, human respect, pleasure, power, and influence. Help me to become deaf to these voices and more attentive to your voice, which calls me to choose the narrow road to life.

I know that Lent is going to be a very hard time for me. The choice for your way has to be made every moment of my life. I have to choose thoughts that are your thoughts, words that are your words, and actions that are your actions. There are no times or places without choices. And I know how deeply I resist choosing you.

Please, Lord, be with me at every moment and in every place. Give me the strength and the courage to live this season faithfully, so that, when Easter comes, I will be able to taste with joy the new life which you have prepared for me.

Amen.

Choosing Joy

(Thursday, February 13)

In the first reading of the Eucharist today I heard: "I am offering you life or death . . . choose life, then, so that you and your descendents may live in the love of Yahweh your God, obeying his voice, holding fast to him" (Deuteronomy 30:19–20).

How do I choose life? I am becoming aware that there are few moments without the opportunity to choose, since death and life are always before me. One aspect of choosing life is choosing joy. Joy is life-giving, but sadness brings death. A sad heart is a heart in which something is dying. A joyful heart is a heart in which something new is being born.

I think that joy is much more than a mood. A mood invades us. We do not choose a mood. We often find ourselves in a happy or depressed mood without knowing where it comes from. The spiritual life is a life beyond moods. It is a life in which we choose joy and do not allow ourselves to become victims of passing feelings of happiness or depression.

I am convinced that we can choose joy. Every moment we can decide to respond to an event or a person with joy instead of sadness. When we truly believe that God is life and only life, then nothing need have the power to draw us into the sad realm of death. To choose joy does not mean to choose happy feelings or an artificial atmosphere of hilarity. But it does mean the determination to let whatever takes place bring us one step closer to the God of life.

Maybe this is what is so important about quiet moments of meditation and prayer. They allow me to take a critical look at my moods and to move from victimization to free choice.

This morning I woke up somewhat depressed. I could not find any reason for it. Life just felt empty, useless, fatiguing. I felt invaded by somber spirits. I realized that this mood was lying to me. Life is not meaningless. God has created life as an expression of love. It helped me to know this, even though I could not feel it. Based on this knowledge, I could again choose joy. This choice means simply to act according to the truth. The depressed mood is still there. I cannot just force it out of my heart. But at least I can unmask it as being untrue and thus prevent it from becoming the ground for my actions.

I am called to be joyful. It gives much consolation to know that I can choose joy.

All Is Well Around the Münster

(Saturday, February 15)

Saturday afternoon, 5 P.M. at the Münster. It is very still on the Münster square. A very light, hardly noticeable snow falls softly on the cobblestones. The houses standing around the Münster form a quiet, peaceful community, like children sitting around a bonfire listening to a story. There is hardly any noise. The stores have been closed since noon. No cars, no shouting voices, not even the noise of children playing. Here and there I see people crossing the empty snow-covered square and entering the church.

The sun has gone down, but it is not fully dark yet. The grey sky is filled with little white dots. A few lights burn outside the guesthouses, inviting people to come in and drink some wine or eat some hearty food.

I look up at the tower of the Münster. She tells her story without words, a wise old grandmother smiling at her grandchildren, who say, "Tell us that story again." Beams of light cover her full length, and through the open spire a warm inner light shines forth from her. I look and feel comforted and consoled. She seems to say, "Do not worry so much. God loves you."

In the church it is dark. But there is an island of light in front of the large statue of the Virgin and Child. The flames of hundreds of small candles make the light look like something alive and moving. A few people are standing there praying with closed eyes.

In the little side chapels surrounding the main altar priests are hearing confessions. People come and go silently. I kneel in front of one of the priests to confess my sins. He listens to me attentively and speaks gentle words about the importance of being joyful at all times. As he absolves me in the name of the Father, the Son, and the Holy Spirit, I feel some of the joy he spoke about.

I pray for a while in front of the statue of the Virgin. Then I walk home with a heart full of peace. It has become very dark now. The glowing tower still stands there and smiles at me. All is well.

A Happy Reunion

(Wednesday, February 19)

Tonight at 7 P.M. Jonas arrived from Boston! A few weeks ago he called and said he would like to spend the last few days of my stay in Germany with me. I was overjoyed.

Jonas was able to take a few days of vacation and had found a cheap flight to Europe. This morning he arrived in Brussels and came to Freiburg by train via Cologne. It continues to amaze me how small the world has become. Last night we were still thousands of miles away from each other. Tonight we had supper together, talked about a thousand things, and prayed together in the chapel. We are looking forward to a few peaceful days together.

Letting Go of Divisions

(Friday, February 21)

This morning Jonas and I read in the Gospel Jesus' words: "If you are bringing your gift to the altar, and there you remember that your brother or sister has something against you, leave your gift in front of the altar; go at once and make peace with your brother, and then come back and offer your gift" (Matthew 5:23–24).

These words have stayed with us for the whole day. I realize that there are still many people with whom I am not fully at peace. When I think back on the friendships, encounters, and confrontations of the past, I realize that islands of anger, bitterness, and resentment still lie hidden in my heart. And when I bring to mind all whom I personally know or about whom I have heard or read, I know how I divide them between those who are for me and those who are against me, those whom I like and those whom I do not like, those whom I want to be with and those whom I try to avoid at all costs. My inner life is so filled with opinions, judgments, and prejudices about my "brothers and sisters" that real peace is still far away.

As I think about Jesus' words, I know that I must let go of all these divisive emotions and thoughts so that I can truly experience peace with all of God's people. This means an unrestrained willingness to forgive and let go of old fears, bitterness, resentment, anger, and lust, and thus find reconciliation.

In this way, I can be a real peacemaker. My inner peace can be a source of peace for all I meet. I can then offer gifts on the altar of God as a testimony to this peace with my brothers and sisters.

I have to start thinking about concrete ways to make peace with my brothers and sisters who have something against me. What do I have to lose? To make peace is to free myself from my easy judgments so that I can love my enemy and the God who holds me and my enemies together in the palm of his hand.

Today I experience deep gratitude for the friendship between Jonas and me. It is the visible fruit of our peacemaking in November.

God's Light Shining Through Our Bodies

(Strasbourg; Sunday, February 23)

At 8 A.M. Franz and Robert Johna drove Jonas and me to Strasbourg. At 11 A.M. we participated in the eucharistic celebration in the cathedral. The dean of the cathedral invited me to concelebrate with him. A tall young Franciscan priest serving as chaplain at the University of Strasbourg was giving the sermon.

After the Gospel reading of the transfiguration, the Franciscan climbed the richly carved pulpit in the middle of the cathedral. All the worshipers turned their chairs around so that they could see him and listen attentively. He spoke about the transfiguration not only of Jesus, but of all creation. As he spoke he pointed to the brilliant yellow, white, and blue rose window above the cathedral entrance. He said, "Though this is a great piece of art, we can only see its full splendor when the sun shines through it." Then he explained how our bodies, the work of our hands, and all that exists can shine with splendor only when we let God's light shine through them. As he spoke, I kept looking at the magnificent rose window—at thirteen meters across, the largest ever made—and I had a new sense of the transfiguration that took place on Mount Tabor: God's light bursting forth from the body of Jesus. Six centuries ago a rose-window was made that today helps me to see the glory of Christ in a new way. Again I felt part of the long journey of the people of God through the centuries. There was much that was old and much that was new. There were statues of saints, kings, and queens of long ago. There were also friendly priests in dungarees and turtlenecks, women acolytes, and many cars parked around the cathedral. I could see history moving. But again and again there recurred that same story on the second Sunday of Lent, the story of the transfiguration of Jesus.

At 12:45 P.M. the moment of departure arrived. As Jonas and I waved to Franz and Robert from the slowly moving train, I felt we had become part of something deep and lasting of which the cathedral of Strasbourg had been only one last reminder.

16

The Descending Way

Friends Meet Friends

(Trosly; Monday, February 24)

A day full of hellos and good-byes back at Trosly. Madame Vanier, Paquita, Barbara, Simone, Mirella, and many others welcomed us warmly and showed sincere joy at seeing both of us again. The most important event of the day for me was a lunch with Jonas and Nathan. Although Jonas had met Nathan during his last visit, they had not come to know each other well. Since my friendship with Nathan has grown so quickly and deeply during the past few months, I was eager to give Jonas and Nathan a chance to get to know each other better. Friendships need to be shared; I was very glad that Jonas could spend some more time with Nathan before his return to Boston. We spoke mostly about friendship and its importance in our lives. What I remember most was our discussion about the importance of confessing our struggles to each other, not just when they became unbearable, but very early on. Jonas said, "The demons love darkness and hiddenness. Inner fears and struggles which remain isolated develop great power over us. But when we talk about them in a spirit of trust, then they can be looked at and dealt with. Once brought into the light of mutual love, demons lose their power and quickly leave us."

I realized that what Jonas said was the core of the sacrament of penance. Through confession and forgiveness we can experience the healing, reconciling, and recreating power of God's love. I was glad to realize that what I had learned through the practice of the sacrament of confession had implications for a life of faithful friendship. Just as the celebration of the Eucharist calls us to gratitude at all times and places, so, too, does the celebration of the sacrament of penance call us to a way of living in which we are always willing to confess and forgive.

When I took Jonas to the railroad station tonight and waved good-bye to him, I felt deeply grateful for the bonds of friendship that had grown during the last months. These bonds make large distances seem small and heavy burdens feel light.

On Slowing Down the Sun

(Tuesday, March 4)

Since returning from Freiburg I have been busy with countless tasks, yet feeling that nothing is being accomplished. From early in the morning to late at night I have been occupied with letters, phone calls, visits, meetings, and other seemingly urgent things. But I have not done much of what I think I am here for: praying and writing. I have kept up with my morning hour of meditation, I have celebrated the Eucharist every day, I have said my evening prayers, but I haven't felt any vitality. I have been somewhat wooden, hard, and dry! And I have let the days go by just keeping up with the little things. I found a suitcase filled with letters which had piled up during my six weeks in Germany. Wonderful, lovely letters. But as I start reading and answering them the hours flow by and the days melt away.

I am frustrated because in the midst of this busy life I keep having ideas, insights, and feelings which I want to pour out on paper. And the more ideas, insights, and feelings I have, the more frustrated I get: too many to hold, too much to remember, too much to save for later. I want to write now, not later.

One friend wrote in his letter, "I hope you find time to write, but don't take yourself too seriously!" Maybe I have to smile a little about my obsessions and compulsions. Maybe I have to trust that there will be time when there has to be. Meanwhile, I keep protesting to God that the days are created so short. I keep saying, "Please, Lord, slow that sun down!" But it keeps going as always, round and round and round. No faster, no slower, twenty-four hours each day!

Peter called today and said that the magazine *America* had rejected the meditation on the Pentecost icon I wrote in Freiburg. I felt it was the best of the four icon meditations I had written, but the editor of *America* wrote in a short note, "It is not up to the standard that we are used to from Henri Nouwen." Well that might slow *me* down a little instead of the sun! It was a good way to help me take myself less seriously.

Maybe this is one way of reminding myself that I cannot make myself holy. Holiness is a gift from God, not something I can ever claim as the result of my own doing.

Life is humbling, very humbling. I have to let it be that way. Someone said today, "We need a lot of humiliation for a little bit of humility."

Staying Connected with Jesus

(Wednesday, March 12)

Today in the Gospel reading of the liturgy, Jesus reveals that everything he does is done in relationship with his Father: "The Son can do nothing by himself; he can do only what he sees the Father doing; and whatever the Father does the Son does too" (John 5:19).

After the intense experience of disconnectedness I had yesterday, Jesus' words have a special meaning for me. I must live in an ongoing relationship with Jesus and through him with the Father. This relationship is the core of the spiritual life. This relationship prevents my life from being consumed by "keeping up" with things. This relationship prevents my days from becoming boring, fatiguing, draining, depressing, and frustrating.

If all that I do can become more and more an expression of my participation in God's life of total giving and receiving in love, everything else will be blessed and will lose its fragmented quality. This does not mean that everything will become easy and harmonious. There will still be much agony, but when connected with God's own agony, even my agony can lead to life.

I guess it all boils down to a call to pray unceasingly.

I Love Jesus, but . . .

(Saturday, March 15)

The Gospel today reveals that Jesus not only had good, faithful friends willing to follow him wherever he went and fierce enemies who couldn't wait to get rid of him, but also many sympathizers who were attracted, but afraid at the same time.

The rich young man loved Jesus but couldn't give up his wealth to follow him. Nicodemus admired Jesus but was afraid to lose the respect of his own colleagues. I am becoming more and more aware of the importance of looking at these fearful sympathizers because that is the group I find myself mostly gravitating toward.

I love Jesus but want to hold on to my own friends even when they do not lead me closer to Jesus. I love Jesus but want to hold on to my own independence even when that independence brings me no real freedom. I love Jesus but do not want to lose the respect of my professional colleagues, even though I know that their respect does not make me grow spiritually. I love Jesus but do not want to give up my writing plans, travel plans, and speaking plans, even when these plans are often more to my glory than to the glory of God.

So I am like Nicodemus, who came by night, said safe things about Jesus to his colleagues, and expressed his guilt by bringing to the grave more myrrh and aloes than needed or desired.

To his colleagues, the Pharisees, Nicodemus said, "our Law does not allow us to pass judgment on anyone without first giving him a hearing and discovering what he is doing" (John 7:51). These are careful words. They are spoken to people who hate Jesus. But they are spoken on their terms. They say, "Even if you hate Jesus and desire to kill him, do not lose your dignity, follow your own rules." Nicodemus said it to save Jesus, but he didn't want to lose his friends. It didn't work. He was ridiculed by his friends: "Are you a Galilean too? Go into the matter, and see for yourself: prophets do not arise from Galilee!" His personal and professional identity are attacked.

It is such a familiar scene. I have spoken like Nicodemus in episcopal committees and faculty meetings many times. Instead of speaking directly about my love for Jesus, I make a smart remark suggesting that maybe my friends should look at another side of the question. They usually respond by saying I have not studied my sources well enough, or that I seem to have some sentimental attachment that got in the way of a truly professional approach. Those who have said these things have had the power of right thinking and thus forced me to silence. But it has been fear that has prevented me from speaking from the heart and risking rejection.

Nicodemus deserves all my attention. Can I stay a Pharisee and follow Jesus too? Doesn't that condemn me to bringing costly spices to the grave when it is too late?

On Retreat

(Nevers; Monday, March 17)

Tonight I am in Nevers, five hours by car from Trosly. I am here to make a "covenant retreat" with Jean Vanier and forty L'Arche assistants. We will be here the whole week to pray, listen to Jean's reflections on living the Gospel at L'Arche, share ideas and experiences, and explore the bond we have with handicapped people.

The Cry of the Poor

(Tuesday, March 18)

Two themes run through Jean's reflections: the descending way of God and the call to find God not just by serving the poor, but by *becoming* poor. God, who created the universe in all its splendor, decided to reveal to us the mystery of the divine life by becoming flesh in a young woman living in a humble village on one of the small planets of God's own creation. Jesus' life is marked by an always deeper choice of what is small, humble, poor, rejected, and despised. The poor are the preferred dwelling place of God. Thus they have become the way to meet God.

Handicapped people are not only poor; they also reveal to us our own poverty. Their primal call is an anguished cry: "Do you love me?" and "Why have you forsaken me?" When we are confronted with that cry, so visible in those people who have no capacity to hide behind their intellectual defenses, we are forced to look at our own terrible loneliness and our own primal cry. We hear this cry everywhere in our world. Jews, blacks, Palestinians, refugees, and many others all cry out, "Why is there no place for us, why are we rejected, why are we pushed away?" Jesus has lived this primal cry with us. "My God, my God, why have you forsaken me?" He, who came from God to lead us to God, suffered the deepest anguish a human being can suffer, the anguish of being left alone, rejected, forgotten, abandoned by the one who is the source of all life.

L'Arche is founded on this cry of the poor. L'Arche is a response to the cry of Jesus, which is the cry of all who suffer anguish and who wonder if there can be any real bond with anyone. Jesus came to reunite, to heal, to form bonds, to reconcile. He shared our anguish so that through our anguish we would be able to find the way back to God. Jesus descended to ascend. "He emptied himself . . . he was humbler yet, even to accepting death, death on a cross . . . for this God raised him high and gave him the name which is above all other names" (Philippians 2:7–9).

L'Arche Built upon the Body

(Thursday, March 20)

One of the most important things that Jean Vanier is saying to me during this retreat is that L'Arche is built upon the body and not upon the word. This helps to explain my struggle in coming to L'Arche. Until now my whole life has been centered around the word: learning, teaching, reading, writing, speaking. Without the word, my life is unthinkable. A good day is a day with a good conversation, a good lecture given or heard, a good book read, or a good article written. Most of my joys and pains are connected with words.

L'Arche, however, is built not on words, but on the body. The community of L'Arche is a community formed around the wounded bodies of handicapped people. Feeding, cleaning, touching, holding—this is what builds the community. Words are secondary. Most handicapped people have few words to speak, and many do not speak at all. It is the language of the body that counts most.

"The Word became flesh." That is the center of the Christian message. Before the Incarnation, the relationship between body and word was unclear. Often the body was seen as a hindrance to the full realization of what the word wanted to express. But Jesus confronts us with the word that can be seen, heard, and touched. The body thus becomes the way to know the word and to enter into relationship with the word. The body of Jesus becomes the way to life. "He who eats my body and drinks my blood will have eternal life."

I feel a deep resistance against this way. Somehow I have come to think about eating, drinking, washing, and dressing as so many necessary preconditions for reading, speaking, teaching, or writing. Somehow the pure word was the real thing for me. Time spent with "material" things was necessary but needed to be kept to a minimum. But at L'Arche, that is where all the attention goes. At L'Arche the body is the place where the word is met. It is in relationship to the wounded body of the handicapped person that I must learn to discover God.

This is very hard for me. I still find a long meal in the middle of the day a waste of time. I still think that I have more important things to do than to set the table, eat slowly, wash the dishes, and set the table again. I think, "Surely we must eat, but the work which comes after is what counts." But L'Arche cannot be endured with this mind set.

I wonder when and how I will learn to fully live the Incarnation. I suppose that only the handicapped people themselves will be able to show me the way. I must trust that God will send me the teachers I need.

The Covenant

(Friday, March 21)

This is a covenant retreat. A covenant retreat is a retreat in which those who have lived and worked at L'Arche for some years are invited to announce publicly the covenant with Jesus and the poor which has grown in them. Announcing the covenant is not a vow, nor even a promise. It is a public acknowledgement that a special bond with the poor and with Jesus, who lives in the poor, has developed over the years.

This covenant is something new in the Church. It does not make you a member of an order or religious association. It does not incorporate you into an institution. It does not give you special status or privilege. It does not bind you to stay at L'Arche and continue working with mentally handicapped people. The covenant is something much more intimate, personal, and hidden. It is a bonding that is not created, but acknowledged as having in fact taken place. It is a work of God that is announced to brothers and sisters of the same community. The announcement is a witness to what God is doing through Jesus in people who work with the poor, and is thus a sign of hope and encouragement for all who search to be faithful to the Gospel.

It is very clear that I am far from announcing the covenant myself. I have just come to know L'Arche and have not yet lived full-time in a foyer. I know something of the spirituality of L'Arche, but that knowledge has not yet become flesh in me. I am drawn to various handicapped people and assistants, but a deep bonding with them has not yet taken place. I need to "live L'Arche" much longer and more deeply, so that the covenant can grow in me; only then can I announce it to others as a gift freely given to me.

This retreat is making me aware of how fragmented my life

has been so far. There has been so much individualism, competition, rivalry, privileges, favors, and exceptions in my way of living that few deep and lasting bonds could grow. But Jesus came to create bonds, and living in, with, and through Jesus means discovering these bonds in myself and revealing them to others. There are bonds between handicapped people and their assistants, between handicapped people and their families, between handicapped people and their neighbors, and most of all between handicapped people and their fellow handicapped people. There are bonds between Catholic Christians and Protestant Christians, between Christians and those who believe in God, between those who believe in God and all who share the same humanity. There are bonds between human beings and animals, between human beings and the earth, and between human beings and the whole universe. Satan divides, pulls apart, fragments, and disrupts. Jesus unites, reconciles, heals, and restores. Wherever we experience bonding, there is Jesus. He came to invite us to enter with him into that intimate covenant that exists between himself and his Father. This is the bond that is the source and goal of all bonding. All creation is called to unity with God in and through Jesus, whose whole being is being bonded in love to his divine Father.

Announcing the Covenant

(Saturday, March 22)

It was very moving to see the retreatants stand in front of the altar and announce their covenant with Jesus and the poor. As I looked into the faces of my brothers and sisters who had chosen the downward way of Jesus, I realized that they would give me the strength to announce the same covenant when the time for it comes.

The more I ponder what Jean Vanier has said, the more I realize how seemingly impossible is the way he calls me to go.

Everything in me wants to move upward. Downward mobility with Jesus goes radically against my inclinations, against the advice of the world surrounding me, and against the culture of which I am a part. In choosing to become poor with the poor at L'Arche, I still hope to gain praise for that choice. Wherever I turn I am confronted with my deep-seated resistance against following Jesus on his way to the cross and my countless ways of avoiding poverty, whether material, intellectual, or emotional. Only Jesus, in whom the fullness of God dwells, could freely and fully choose to be completely poor.

I see clearer now that choosing to become poor is choosing to make every part of my journey with Jesus. Becoming truly poor is impossible, but "nothing is impossible to God" (Luke 1:37). In and through Jesus I believe that the way to true poverty will open itself to me. After all, it is not *my* poverty that has any value, but only God's poverty, which becomes visible through my life.

This sounds unreal, but when I saw the men and women who announced their covenant with Jesus and the poor, I saw how real this downward way of Jesus is and how, if I go this way, I go not alone, but as a member of the "body of Jesus." Seldom have I experienced so directly the difference between individual heroism and communal obedience. Whenever I think about becoming poor as something I must accomplish, I become depressed. But as soon as I realize that my brothers and sisters call me to go this way with them in obedience to Jesus, I am filled with hope and joy.

This afternoon we all returned to our different communities and foyers. It was a very hard week for me, but full of blessings.

17

Passion, Death, and Resurrection

Being Handed Over

(Trosly; Tuesday, March 25)

Jesus, sitting at table with his disciples, said, "One of you will betray me" (John 13:21). I read this today in the Gospel.

As I look more closely at Jesus' words as they are written in Greek, a better translation would be "One of you will hand me over." The term *paradidomi* means "to give over, to hand over, to give into the hands of." It is an important term not only to express what Judas did, but also what God did. Paul writes, ". . . he did not spare his own Son, but 'handed him over' for the sake of all of us" (Romans 8:32).

If we translate Judas's action as "to betray," as applied to Judas, we do not fully express the mystery because Judas is described as being an instrument of God's work. That is why Jesus said, "The Son of Man is going to his fate, as the scriptures say he will, but alas for the man by whom the Son of Man is betrayed [handed over]" (Matthew 26:24).

This moment when Jesus is handed over to those who do with him as they please is a turning point in Jesus' ministry. It is turning from action to passion. After years of teaching, preaching, healing, and moving to wherever he wanted to go, Jesus is handed over to the caprices of his enemies. Things are now no longer done *by* him, but *to* him. He is flagellated, crowned with thorns, spat at, laughed at, stripped, and nailed naked to a cross. He is a passive victim, subject to other people's actions. From the moment Jesus is handed over, his passion begins, and through this passion he fulfills his vocation.

It is important for me to realize that Jesus fulfills his mission not by what he does, but by what is done to him. Just as with everyone else, most of my life is determined by what is done to me and thus is passion. And because most of my life is passion, things being done to me, only small parts of my life are determined by what I think, say, or do. I am inclined to protest against this and to want all to be action, originated by me. But the truth is that my passion is a much greater part of my life than my action. Not to recognize this is self-deception and not to embrace my passion with love is self-rejection.

It is good news to know that Jesus is handed over to passion, and through his passion accomplishes his divine task on earth. It is good news for a world passionately searching for wholeness.

Jesus' words to Peter remind me that Jesus' transition from action to passion must also be ours if we want to follow his way. He says, "When you were young you put on your own belt and walked where you liked; but when you grow old you will stretch out your hands, and somebody else will put a belt round you and take you where you would rather not go" (John 21:18).

I, too, have to let myself be "handed over" and thus fulfill my vocation.

Running Away or Returning

(Wednesday, March 26)

During this week Judas and Peter present me with the choice between running away from Jesus in despair or returning to him in hope. Judas betrayed Jesus and hanged himself. Peter denied Jesus and returned to him in tears.

Sometimes despair seems an attractive choice, solving everything in the negative. The voice of despair says, "I sin over and over again. After endless promises to myself and others to do better next time, I find myself back again in the old dark places. Forget about trying to change. I have tried for years. It didn't work and it will never work. It is better that I get out of people's way, be forgotten, no longer around, dead."

This strangely attractive voice takes all uncertainties away and puts an end to the struggle. It speaks unambiguously for the darkness and offers a clear-cut negative identity.

But Jesus came to open my ears to another voice that says, "I am your God, I have molded you with my own hands, and I love what I have made. I love you with a love that has no limits, because I love you as I am loved. Do not run away from me. Come back to me—not once, not twice, but always again. You are my child. How can you ever doubt that I will embrace you again, hold you against my breast, kiss you and let my hands run through your hair? I am your God—the God of mercy and compassion, the God of pardon and love, the God of tenderness and care. Please do not say that I have given up on you, that I cannot stand you anymore, that there is no way back. It is not true. I so much want you to be with me. I so much want you to be close to me. I know all your thoughts. I hear all your words. I see all of your actions. And I love you because you are beautiful, made in my own image, an expression of my most intimate love. Do not judge yourself. Do not condemn yourself.

Do not reject yourself. Let my love touch the deepest, most hidden corners of your heart and reveal to you your own beauty, a beauty that you have lost sight of, but which will become visible to you again in the light of my mercy. Come, come, let me wipe your tears, and let my mouth come close to your ear and say to you, 'I love you, I love you, I love you.' "

This is the voice that Jesus wants us to hear. It is the voice that calls us always to return to the one who has created us in love and wants to re-create us in mercy. Peter heard that voice and trusted it. As he let that voice touch his heart, tears came—tears of sorrow and tears of joy, tears of remorse and tears of peace, tears of repentance and tears of gratitude.

It is not easy to let the voice of God's mercy speak to us because it is a voice asking for an always open relationship, one in which sins are acknowledged, forgiveness received, and love renewed. It does not offer us a solution, but a friendship. It does not take away our problems, but promises not to avoid them. It does not tell us where it all will end, but assures us that we will never be alone. A true relationship is hard work because loving is hard work, with many tears and many smiles. But it is God's work and worth every part of it.

O Lord, my Lord, help me to listen to your voice and choose your mercy.

Washing the Feet of the Poor

(Thursday, March 27)

This afternoon I took the train to Paris to celebrate the Holy Thursday liturgy with the L'Arche community, "Nomaste." It was a very moving celebration. We gathered in the community room of Nomaste. There were about forty people. In his welcome, the director of the community, Toni Paoli, expressed his vision that L'Arche should be not simply a comfortable place for handicapped people, but a Christian community in which people serve one another in the name of Jesus. After the Gospel reading, he again proclaimed his deep love for Jesus. Then he stood up and washed the feet of four members of his community.

After the Eucharist, a rice dish, bread, and wine were brought and put on the altar. In silence, deepened by three short Gospel readings about God's love, we shared this simple food.

Sitting in the basement room in Paris surrounded by forty poor people, I was struck again by the way Jesus concluded his active life. Just before entering on the road of his passion he washed the feet of his disciples and offered them his body and blood as food and drink. These two acts belong together. They are both an expression of God's determination to show us the fullness of his love. Therefore John introduces the story of the washing of the disciples' feet with the words: "Jesus . . . having loved those who were his in the world, loved them to the end" (John 13:1).

What is even more astonishing is that on both occasions Jesus commands us to do the same. After washing his disciples' feet, Jesus says, "I have given you an example so that you may copy what I have done to you" (John 13:15). After giving himself as food and drink, he says, "Do this in remembrance of me" (Luke 22:19). Jesus calls us to continue his mission of revealing the perfect love of God in this world. He calls us to total self-giving. He does not want us to keep anything for ourselves. Rather, he wants our love to be as full, as radical, and as complete as his own. He wants us to bend ourselves to the ground and touch the places in each other that most need washing. He also wants us to say to each other, "Eat of me and drink of me." By this complete mutual nurturing, he wants us to become one body and one spirit, united by the love of God.

When Toni spoke to his community about his love for Jesus, and when I saw how he washed their feet and gave them the bread and wine, it seemed as if—for the moment—I saw a glimpse of the new kingdom Jesus came to bring. Everybody in the room knew how far he or she was from being a perfect expression of God's love. But everybody was also willing to make a step in the direction to which Jesus pointed.

It was an evening in Paris I will not easily forget.

The Immense Suffering
of Humanity

(Friday, March 28)

Good Friday: day of the cross, day of suffering, day of hope, day of abandonment, day of victory, day of mourning, day of joy, day of endings, day of beginnings.

During the liturgy at Trosly, Père Thomas and Père Gilbert, a former assistant who has become a priest for the L'Arche community in Trosly, took the huge cross that hangs behind the altar from the wall and held it so that the whole community could come and kiss the dead body of Christ.

They all came, more than four hundred people—handicapped men and women and their assistants and friends. Everybody seemed to know very well what they were doing: expressing their love and gratitude for him who gave his life for them. As they were crowding around the cross and kissing the feet and the head of Jesus, I closed my eyes and could see his sacred body stretched out and crucified upon our planet earth. I saw the immense suffering of humanity during the centuries: people killing each other; people dying from starvation and epidemics; people driven from their homes; people sleeping on the streets of large cities; people clinging to each other in desperation; people flagellated, tortured, burned, and mutilated; people alone in locked flats, in prison dungeons, in labor camps; people craving a gentle word, a friendly letter, a consoling embrace, people—children, teenagers, adults, middle-aged, and elderly—all crying out with an anguished voice: "My God, my God, why have you forsaken us?"

Imagining the naked, lacerated body of Christ stretched out

over our globe, I was filled with horror. But as I opened my eyes I saw Jacques, who bears the marks of suffering in his face, kiss the body with passion and tears in his eyes. I saw Ivan carried on Michael's back. I saw Edith coming in her wheelchair. As they came—walking or limping, seeing or blind, hearing or deaf—I saw the endless procession of humanity gathering around the sacred body of Jesus, covering it with their tears and their kisses, and slowly moving away from it comforted and consoled by such great love. There were signs of relief; there were smiles breaking through tear-filled eyes; there were hands in hands and arms in arms. With my mind's eye I saw the huge crowds of isolated, agonizing individuals walking away from the cross together, bound by the love they had seen with their own eyes and touched with their own lips. The cross of horror became the cross of hope, the tortured body became the body that gives new life; the gaping wounds became the source of forgiveness, healing, and reconciliation. Père Thomas and Père Gilbert were still holding the cross. The last people came, knelt, and kissed the body, and left. It was quiet, very quiet.

Père Gilbert then gave me a large chalice with the consecrated bread and pointed to the crowd standing around the altar.

I took the chalice and moved among those whom I had seen coming to the cross; looked at their hungry eyes and said, "The body of Christ . . . the body of Christ . . . the body of Christ" countless times. The small community became all of humanity, and I knew that all I needed to say my whole life long was, "Take and eat. This is the body of Christ."

A Promise of Resurrection

(Saturday, March 29)

Easter vigil. The Lord is risen indeed. They shouted it in French, German, English, Spanish, Portuguese, Italian, Dutch, and Arabic. There were bells, alleluias, smiles, laughter, and a deep sense that there is hope. This community of handicapped people and their assistants was loudly proclaiming that Christ's body did not remain in the tomb, but was raised to new life, and that our own bodies will join him in glory.

While all this joy was filling the chapel, I saw that Nathan stood up with Philippe in his arms and left the church. Philippe's body is severely distorted. He cannot speak, walk, dress, or feed himself and needs help every second of his waking hours. He had been lying in an assistant's lap, quietly sleeping. But when the celebration became more lively he started to howl, an anguished howl coming from deep down in his being. After a while his howls became so intense and loud that Nathan had to carry him to the car and drive him home.

When I saw Philippe in Nathan's arms I suddenly realized what we were proclaiming on this Easter vigil. Philippe's body is a body destined to a new life, a resurrected life. In his new body he will carry the signs of his suffering, just as Jesus carried the wounds of the crucifixion into his glory. And yet he will no longer be suffering, but will join the saints around the altar of the lamb.

Still, the celebration of the resurrection of the body is also the celebration of the daily care given to the bodies of these handicapped men and women. Washing and feeding, pushing wheelchairs, carrying, kissing, and caressing—these are all ways in which these broken bodies are made ready for the moment of a new life. Not only their wounds but also the care given them will remain visible in the resurrection.

It is a great and powerful mystery. Philippe's poor distorted body will one day be buried and return to dust. But he will rise again on the day of the resurrection of the dead. He will rise from the grave with a new body and will show gloriously the pain he suffered and the love he received. It will not be just *a* body. It will be *his* body, a new body, a body that can be touched but is no longer subject to torture and destruction. His passion will be over.

What a faith! What a hope! What a love! The body is not a prison to escape from, but a temple in which God already dwells, and in which God's glory will be fully manifested on the day of the resurrection.

An Intimate Event

(Sunday, March 30)

Easter morning. A very simple, quiet Eucharist around the table in Madame Vanier's dining room. There were five of us: Madame Vanier, Sue Hall from Canada, Elizabeth Buckley from the United States, Liz Emergy from England, and myself. A small group of friends happy to be together.

After the Gospel we spoke together about the resurrection. Liz, who works with many anguished people, said, "We have to keep rolling away the large stones that prevent people from coming out of their graves." Elizabeth, who lives with four handicapped people in a L'Arche foyer, said, "After the resurrection Jesus had breakfast again with his friends and showed them the importance of the small, ordinary things of life." Sue, who is wondering if she might be called to go to Honduras and work with the L'Arche community there, said, "It is such a comfort to know that Jesus' wounds remain visible in his risen body. Our wounds are not taken away, but become sources of hope to others."

As everyone spoke, I felt very close to the Easter event. It was not a spectacular event forcing people to believe. Rather, it was an event for the friends of Jesus, for those who had known him, listened to him, and believed in him. It was a very intimate event: a word here, a gesture there, and a gradual awareness that something new was being born—small, hardly noticed, but with the potential to change the face of the earth. Mary of Magdala heard her name. John and Peter saw the empty grave. Jesus' friends felt their hearts burn in encounters that find expression in the remarkable words "He is risen." All had remained the same, while all had changed.

The five of us, sitting in a circle around the table with a little bread and a little wine, speaking softly about the way we were recognizing him in our lives, knew deep in our hearts that for us too all had changed, while all had remained the same. Our struggles are not ended. On Easter morning we can still feel the pains of the world, the pains of our family and friends, the pains of our hearts. They are still there and will be there for a long time. Still, all is different because we have met Jesus and he has spoken to us.

There was a simple, quiet joy among us and a deep sense of being loved by a love that is stronger, much stronger, than death.

Knowing and Loving

(Tuesday, April 1)

Today we heard the story of the encounter between Jesus and Mary of Magdala, two people who love each other. Jesus says, "Mary." She recognizes him and says, " 'Rabboni,' which means Master" (John 20:16). This simple and deeply moving story brings me in touch with my fear as well as my desire to be known. When Jesus calls Mary by her name, he is doing much more than speaking the word by which everybody knows her, for her name signifies her whole being. Jesus knows Mary of Magdala. He knows her story: her sin and her virtue, her fears and her love, her anguish and her hope. He knows every part of her heart. Nothing in her is hidden from him. He knows her even more deeply and more fully than she knows herself. Therefore, when he utters her name he brings about a profound event. Mary suddenly realizes that the one who truly knows her truly loves her.

I am always wondering if people who know every part of me, including my deepest, most hidden thoughts and feelings, really do love me. Often I am tempted to think that I am loved only as I remain partially unknown. I fear that the love I receive is conditional and then say to myself, "If they really knew me, they would not love me." But when Jesus calls Mary by name he speaks to her entire being. She realizes that the one who knows her most deeply is not moving away from her, but is coming to her offering her his unconditional love.

Her response is "Rabboni," "Master." I hear her response as her desire to have Jesus truly be her master, the master of her whole being: her thoughts and feelings, her passion and hope, even her most hidden emotions. I hear her say, "You who know me so fully, come and be my master. I do not want to keep you away from any part of myself. I want you to touch the deepest places of my heart so that I won't belong to anyone but you."

I can see what a healing moment this encounter must have been. Mary feels at once fully known and fully loved. The division between what she feels safe to show and what she does not dare to reveal no longer exists. She is fully seen and she knows that the eyes that see her are the eyes of forgiveness, mercy, love, and unconditional acceptance.

I sense that here, in this simple encounter, we can see a true religious moment. All fear is gone, and all has become love. And how better can this be expressed than by Jesus' words, "go and find my brothers, and tell them: I am ascending to my Father and your Father, to my God and your God" (John 20:17). There is no longer any difference between Jesus and those whom he loves. They are part of the intimacy that Jesus enjoys with his Father. They belong to the same family. They share the same life in God.

What a joy to be fully known and fully loved at the same time! It is the joy of belonging through Jesus to God and being there, fully safe and fully free.

18

Larger Connections

Feeling Caught

(Tuesday, April 8)

A lot of very dark feelings today. Hard to dispel. Most powerful are the feelings of being caught. The powers of darkness have such a grip on me that "coming into the light" seems hardly possible. People leave without saying good-bye, people write saying that I am selfish, people grow angry because I have not written them. People have farewell parties without inviting me, people tell me that the things they promised cannot be done, and so on. Suddenly I feel lost, disconnected, forgotten, left alone, misused, manipulated, confused, angry, resentful, spiteful, and full of self-pity. So little is needed to slip into a depression! I am amazed by the fragility of my emotional balance. The only thing I can do is look at my emotional state with a certain distance and realize how easily everything turns dark.

Happily, the Gospel today has much to tell me—it is the conversation of Jesus with Nicodemus. If there is any conversation I should take seriously, it is this one. So much of me is like Nicodemus, wanting to see the light, but coming to Jesus during the night.

Jesus says to Nicodemus, "though the light has come into the world, people have preferred darkness to the light" (John 3:19). In me I can feel this strange preference for the darkness. It seems as if I resist coming into the light and enjoy staying in my self-made darkness. Jesus offers the light, the truth, the life coming from above. He makes it clear that God wants to pull me away from the darkness; he wants to offer me a solid love to dwell in, a firm ground to stand on, a faithful presence to trust in. But I have to look upward instead of inward, and embrace the gifts that are given.

Yet why all this resistance? Why this powerful attraction to the darkness? Jesus says, "Everybody who does wrong hates the light and avoids it, to prevent his actions from being shown up; but whoever does the truth comes out into the light, so that what he is doing may plainly appear as done in God" (John 3:20–21). That is an answer to my question. I do often prefer my darkness to God's light. I prefer to hang on to my sinful ways because they give me some satisfaction, some sense of self, some feeling of importance. I know quite well that moving into God's light requires me to let go of all these limited pleasures and no longer to see my life as made by me, but as given by God. Living in the light means acknowledging joyfully the truth that all that is good, beautiful, and worthy of praise belongs to God.

It is only a truly God-centered life that will pull me out of my depressions and give me hope. It is a clear path, but a very hard path as well.

Testing the Call

(Wednesday, April 9)

What will going to Daybreak in Canada mean? I do not know, but the letters that I have been receiving indicate that those I most expected to be there might not be there, that the house I expected to live in might not be available, and that the way I expected to live there might not be possible. It is hard for me not to become upset by all this dashing of expectations, but I have to trust that Jesus will be with me more and more as I let go of my riches and join him on the road to poverty. My call is being tested.

The hardest aspect of poverty lies in my not being able to control my own life, but in this Jesus reveals himself to me as my Lord. When I look up at the cross, just as the sick looked up to the serpent that Moses lifted up in the desert (John 3:14), I can expect to be healed and to discover a joy and peace in my heart far beyond the changing moods of everyday living. It is the joy and peace of eternal life that already now can be tasted. I see every day more clearly how much I have to let go of in order to be poor enough to "taste and see" the goodness of the Lord.

Sexuality: Personal and Communal

(Thursday, April 10)

This afternoon I spent time talking with Charles Busch, a friend from Harvard who is visiting me, about chastity. It was an important discussion for me because, as we spoke, we came to see that chastity is a communal virtue.

Often we think about sexuality as a private affair. Sexual fantasies, sexual thoughts, sexual actions are mostly seen as belonging to the private life of a person. But the distinction between the private and the public sphere of life is a false distinction and has created many of the problems we are struggling with in our day. In the Christian life the distinction between a private life (just for me!) and a public life (for the others) does not exist. For the Christian, even the most hidden fantasies, thoughts, feelings, emotions, and actions are a service or a disservice to the community. I can never say, "What I think, feel or do in my private time is nobody else's business." It is everyone's business! The mental and spiritual health of a community depends largely on the way its members live their most personal lives as a service to their fellow human beings.

The complications of living a chaste life are obvious. If I keep my sexual life a hidden life (just for myself), it will gradually be split off from the rest of my life and become a dangerous force. I wonder more and more how much of the sexual compulsions and obsessions that we experience are the result of this privatization of our sexuality. What remains hidden, kept in the dark and uncommunicable, can easily become a destructive force always ready to explode in unexpected moments.

The first step toward chastity rests in knowing that my sexuality is personal *and* communal. I have to dare to realize that I can harm my neighbors not just by what I do or say, but also by what I think. Confession means sharing my inner mental struggles with a trustworthy human being who can receive that confession in the name of the community. This confession can take place in the context of the sacrament of penance, but it does not have to. What is important is that I start becoming accountable to the community for my inner life. This accountability will gradually take away the obsessive and compulsive quality of sexual thoughts and fantasies. The more I give up my private life and convert it into a personal life for which I am responsible to the community, the easier it will become to live a chaste life—because the community formed and kept together by Jesus will transform my selfish desires into a desire to serve the people of God with every part of my being. Once I have confessed my inner life, the community can let the love of Jesus unmask my false desires, expel the demons, and lead me into the light so that, as a child of light, I can witness to the risen Lord. Thus I can live a truly chaste life.

Small People and Small Things

(Friday, April 11)

Being at L'Arche helps one to understand the Gospels in a new way. Today we read the story of the multiplication of bread. "Looking up, Jesus saw the crowds approaching and said to Philip, 'Where can we buy some bread for these people to eat?' . . . Andrew said, 'Here is a boy with five barley loaves and two fish; but what is that among so many?' " (John 6:5–9). For Jesus, the small gifts of an insignificant boy were enough to feed everyone and even have twelve large baskets with scraps left over.

This again is a story about the value of the small people and the small things. The world likes things to be large, big, impressive, and elaborate. God chooses the small things which are overlooked in the big world. Andrew's remark, "five barley loaves and two fish; but what is that among so many?" captures well the mentality of a calculating mind. It sounds as if he says to Jesus, "Can't you count? Five loaves and two fish are simply not enough." But for Jesus they were enough. Jesus took them and gave thanks. That means that he received the small gifts from the small people and acknowledged them as gifts from his heavenly Father. What comes from God must be enough for all the people. Therefore, Jesus distributed the loaves and the fish "as much as they wanted." In giving away the small gifts from the small people, God's generosity is revealed. There is enough, plenty even, for everyone—there are even many leftovers. Here a great mystery becomes visible. What little we give away multiplies. This is the way of God. This is also the way we are called to live our lives. The little love we have, the little knowledge we have, the little advice we have, the little possessions we have, are given to us as gifts of God to be given away. The more we give them away, the more we discover how much there is to give away. The small gifts of God all multiply in the giving.

Something of that mystery is becoming clear to me at L'Arche. How little is L'Arche! The few hundred handicapped people who are cared for in the L'Arche foyers all over the world seem a tiny, insignificant group, considering the countless handicapped people who remain without the necessary care. Statistically, L'Arche makes little sense. And still, something of God is taking place through L'Arche. The little that L'Arche does affects people from the most different countries, religions, races, and social backgrounds. Many are fed by the little food L'Arche is giving away; not just mentally handicapped people, but also the rich, the powerful, the leaders of the church and the society, students, scholars, doctors, lawyers, magistrates, businessmen and women, and people who do not even know what a mental handicap is. They all receive something from L'Arche and are strengthened by it. Thus the miracle of the multiplication of bread continues. It is just a question of having an eye for it.

The Poorest of the Poor

(Saturday, April 12)

Regina, an assistant at L'Arche community in Honduras who came to visit Trosly, had many interesting things to say about life in Honduras. She stressed the low self-esteem of the Honduran people. A small country with a withdrawn, extremely poor, and oppressed Indian population consisting mostly of Mestizos, Honduras has been completely dependent—first on Spain and later on the United States. It now feels threatened by both Nicaragua and El Salvador and greatly fears any signs of revolution. It feels "safe" under the protection of the United States, which has built large military bases there, but it can do nothing without the permission of its powerful protector. Honduras is very, very poor. In contrast to the poor of Haiti, who are liberated blacks from imperial France and often show pride and joy, the poor of Honduras have a much more self-rejecting attitude.

It is not easy for L'Arche to be there. It is hard to find Honduran assistants who can make long-term commitments. They themselves are often part of large, poor families, and most of their energy is used to survive their poverty or, if possible, to escape it. The United States is a land of promise to which they all hope to go and become rich.

Just listening to Regina made me realize how great the poverty of Honduras is. With so little national consciousness and so little pride, living there with handicapped people must be extremely difficult. It is, indeed, living with the poorest of the poor. Still . . . the L'Arche assistants in Honduras are full of peace and joy. They like to be there and hope to remain there. Cathy Judge from Daybreak has visited the community and is full of hope to go and live there. Pilar's letters from Honduras are filled with excitement. Barbara's heart is in Honduras, even though she must stay here in Trosly. Everyone who speaks of the community speaks of it as a most blessed place. Regina herself radiates joy, and it seems that all those who have chosen to live there have found a true treasure. "Happy are the poor of spirit, for the kingdom of heaven is theirs."

I very much hope to visit the Honduras community.

The Interreligious Struggle

(Monday, April 28)

Today I spoke for two hours with Dorothy, an Indian woman who is leader of L'Arche community in Madras, India. She is spending a few months in Trosly to stay in touch with the European communities, to take some rest after many full years of work, and to deepen her own spiritual commitment.

Her description of her life and work in Madras filled me with awe. Moslems, Hindus, and Catholics live in the same house. It is a real struggle to find a common life of worship. In the beginning, when all the assistants were Catholics from Europe, there developed a clearly Catholic liturgical life. But now that Indian assistants from different religious backgrounds have joined, things are much less simple. The Hindu assistants do not have a clear worship ritual, the Moslems do not accept any images, whether Christian or Hindu, and the Catholics do not feel at ease with Hindu or Moslem forms of worship. Moreover, not everyone, whether Catholic, Hindu, or Moslem, is interested in the spiritual life. Some see their work as a paying job that gives them a certain social status and prestige. They do not all share the vision that gave birth to L'Arche.

The development of some common forms of prayer seems impossible. Once one of the handicapped people went to his family home chanting "Oooooomm," the Hindu meditation chant he had learned at L'Arche. His father, a Moslem, was so disturbed that he immediately took his child out of the community.

And yet something very beautiful is happening in India with L'Arche. The handicapped people are bringing people together who otherwise would never meet. They are truly a uniting force. Often we focus on the problems and difficulties that are so obvious and visible. But underneath it all, God, the God of all people, is doing something very beautiful through the little ones.

Dorothy, one of the first Indian assistants, who has been at L'Arche in Madras for more than fourteen years, is herself a true sign of hope. Her vibrant personality, her deep faith in God, and her commitment to L'Arche in India gives me a glimpse of the mystery of God's unifying work through the poor.

19

The Gift of Friendship

Pruning

(Wednesday, April 30)

Jesus said, "I am the true vine, and my Father is the vinedresser. Every branch in me that bears no fruit he cuts away, and every branch that does bear fruit he prunes, to make it bear even more" (John 15:1–2).

These words in today's Gospel open a new perspective on suffering for me. Pruning helps trees to bear more fruit. Even when I bear fruit, even when I do things for God's kingdom, even when people express gratitude for coming to know Jesus through me, I need a lot more pruning. Many unnecessary branches and twigs prevent the vine from bearing all the fruit it can. They have to be clipped off. This is a painful process, all the more so because I do not always know that they are unnecessary. They often seem beautiful, charming, and very alive. But they need to be cut away so that more fruit can grow.

It helps me to think about painful rejections, moments of loneliness, feelings of inner darkness and despair, and lack of support and human affection as God's pruning. I am aware that I might have settled too soon for the few fruits that I can recognize in my life. I might say, "Well, I am doing some good here and there, and I should be grateful for and content with the little good I do." But that might be false modesty and even a form of spiritual laziness. God calls me to more. God wants to prune me. A pruned vine does not look beautiful, but during harvest time it produces much fruit. The great challenge is to continue to recognize God's pruning hand in my life. Then I can avoid resentment and depression and become even more grateful that I am called upon to bear even more fruit than I thought I could. Suffering then becomes a way of purification and allows me to rejoice in its fruits with deep gratitude and without pride.

Brought Together

(Reims; Saturday, May 3)

This afternoon Nathan and I went to Reims for a long weekend.

The plan to spend a few quiet days together away from it all came up when Nathan and I realized that our time in Trosly would soon be over. On May 12 I am leaving on a six-week trip to the United States, Canada, and England, and after that we both have only a few weeks left before we conclude our time in France.

Friendship does not grow strong and deep when you do not give it the time and attention it deserves. My friendship with Nathan has been one of the most sustaining and nurturing aspects of my stay at Trosly.

The great joy of our friendship is that we both deeply feel that it is Jesus who has brought us together so that we would be able to help each other to grow closer to him. Therefore, we want to spend time together in prayer and silence acknowledging that the love we feel for each other is a love that is not of our own making.

So here we are in Reims in the convent of the Sisters of St. Claire. It is a space filled with silence, prayer, and contemplation.

Through the window of my room I see in the distance the majestic Cathedral of Notre Dame rising up in the center of the city. To-morrow we will both see it and pray there.

Thank you, Lord, for the grace of your love, for the grace of friendship, and for the grace of beauty. Amen.

The Cathedral and the Prayer Room

(Sunday, May 4)

In the convent where we are staying there is a small prayer room. It is decorated with a simple stained glass window representing the burning bush, a wooden pillar in which a small tabernacle is carved, some prayer stools and benches, and some small lamps attached to the bamboo-covered walls.

Nathan and I prayed our psalms there and spent some time in silence. It felt very peaceful and restful. Hardly any sounds could be heard.

In the afternoon we went to downtown Reims to visit the Cathedral of Notre Dame. Coming from the small prayer chapel into the majestic nave of the cathedral felt like touching the two extremes of the presence of God in our world. God's hiddenness and God's splendor, God's smallness and God's majesty, God's silence and God's creative word, God's humility and God's trium-phant glory.

Here in this sacred space, built in the thirteenth century, the Saint-King Louis was consecrated (1226), Jeanne d'Arc attended the coronation of Charles VII (1429), Charles X was crowned (1825), and Charles de Gaulle and Konrad Adenauer celebrated the reconciliation between the French and the Germans (1962). So many emotions and feelings, so many tragic and joyous events, so many ugly and beautiful memories, so much pride and so much faith, so much desire for power and so much simple faith.

During World War I, much of the cathedral was burned and destroyed. But in 1937, after twenty years of restoration, it was reopened and reconsecrated by Cardinal Suhard, and today visitors come and gaze at its splendor. After some time trying to absorb some of the cathedral's majesty, Nathan and I sat at a little terrace on the cathedral square and just looked at the three saint-filled entrance portals, at the rosette, at the statues of kings and bishops, and at the two massive towers. Cars and buses came and went, people walked in and out of the entrance doors, some took pictures, others just looked and talked, few prayed. I had a slight headache and wanted to go back to the little prayer room of the convent with the one window of the burning bush, and be there with Jesus and pray. And so we did.

From Opaqueness to Transparency

(Monday, May 5)

As Nathan and I talked together, sharing our struggles and our hopes, it became increasingly clear to me that I know quite well the difference between darkness and light but often do not have the courage to name them by their true names. A strong temptation exists to deal with the darkness as if it were light, and with the light as if it were darkness. The more we talked about our lives, the more I became aware of the inner ambiguities that lead me away from the light and make me hide in dark places.

Knowing Jesus, reading his words, and praying create an increasing clarity about evil and good, sin and grace, Satan and God. This clarity calls me to choose the way to the light fearlessly and straightforwardly. The more I come to know Jesus, the more I also realize how many such choices have to be made and how often. They involve so much more than my public acts. They touch the deepest recesses of the heart, where my most private thoughts and fantasies are hidden.

Reflecting on my life, I saw how opaque it has been. I often did one thing while saying another, said one thing while thinking another, thought one thing while feeling another. I found many examples in which I had even lied to myself. Not seldom have I told myself that I had gone somewhere to help someone but did not allow the truth to enter my mind that I had been driven by much less elevated motivations. I have not acknowledged the subtle desire for power and honor and for emotional and physical satisfaction and have kept playing little games with myself.

How to go from this opaqueness to transparency? A transparent life is a life without moral ambiguities in which heart, mind, and gut are united in choosing for the light. I am discovering the importance of naming the darkness in me. By no longer calling the darkness anything else but darkness, the temptation to keep using it for my own selfish purposes gradually becomes less. As long as I continue to tell lies in the service of the truth, to play death games in the service of life, and to satisfy my impulses in the service of love, I remain hopelessly opaque and become like a preacher fishing for compliments for a sermon on humility.

A hard task is given to me—to call the darkness darkness, evil evil, and the demon demon. By remaining vague I can avoid commitment and drift along in the mainstream of our society. But Jesus does not allow me to stay there. He requires a clear choice for truth, light, and life. When I recognize my countless inner compromises, I may feel guilty and ashamed at first. But when this leads to repentance and a contrite heart, I will soon discover the immense love of God, who came to lead me out of the darkness into the light and who wants to make me into a transparent witness of his love.

I feel grateful for these insights, which emerged from our discussions. Thinking alone is so different from thinking together. As we return to Trosly tomorrow, there will be much good to remember.

Six Ways of Peacemaking

(Trosly; Thursday, May 8)

Today is Ascension Day, a holiday in France and open house at L'Arche in Trosly. Hundreds of friends came to pray and play, to buy L'Arche products, to listen to the local band, and to hear speeches by the director of the community, Alain St. Macary, and Jean Vanier.

The theme of the day was peacemaking. While dozens of little children were running around and making joyful noises, and while many of the handicapped and their assistants were walking around in clown costumes, Jean Vanier offered six ways of being a peacemaker. The loudspeakers were loud enough to let him be heard by those who wanted to hear him. A group of fourteen girls who had heard Jean speak in Lourdes last week had come from Paris for the occasion and welcomed his speech with cheers.

Here are the six points Jean Vanier offered for peacemakers: (1) Respect every individual human being; (2) create space for people to grow and become mature; (3) always stay in dialogue; (4) keep adapting mutual expectations; (5) enjoy the differences among people; (6) always direct your attentions to those who suffer most.

Jean offered these points to help us deal with the many conflicts that keep arising among us. They are the way to peace— whether it be in the family, in the community, or in the world.

After Jean's talk, the band played a few more tunes and people gathered here and there in small groups, exchanging greetings, dancing, singing, or just talking. Then we all walked to the chapel to attend Mass. Against all expectations, the sun kept shining and the heavy clouds drifting by threw only a few drops of rain on us while Jean gave his talk. It was a good Ascension Day!

A Spiritual Strategy

(Saturday, May 10)

More than ever I am aware of the great temptations facing me as I prepare for my journey. On the one hand, I am excited about returning to the United States and Canada, seeing friends, giving talks, counseling people in pain, and being involved again with the "great issues" of the day. On the other hand, I realize how easy it will be to lose touch with Jesus, to become submerged in the countless stimuli coming upon me, and to lose my spiritual balance.

It has helped me to express my fears openly and directly and to ask for spiritual support. Being in the world without being of it involves very hard work. It requires a clear vision of what I want to do and how to do it. It requires a discipline of the eyes, the mind, and the heart. It requires a deep desire, as well as a strong commitment to live without interruptions in the name of Jesus.

I made two concrete promises: to stay close to Jesus by daily prayer and to stay close to my friends by letter and phone. In this way I will be able to remain home even when I travel and to remain in community even when I am alone. Thus I will be able to think, speak, and act not in my own name, but in the name of Jesus and those who sent me.

The Gift of Unity

(Sunday, May 11)

Jesus prays for unity among his disciples and among those who through the teaching of his disciples will come to believe in him.

He says: "May they all be one, just as, Father, you are in me and I in you . . ." (John 17:21).

These words of Jesus reveal the mystery that unity among people is not first of all the result of human effort, but rather a divine gift. Unity among people is a reflection of the unity of God. The desire for unity is deep and strong among people. It is a desire between friends, between married people, between communities, and between countries. Wherever there is a true experience of unity, there is a sense of giftedness. While unity satisfies our deepest need, it cannot be explained by what we say or do. There exists no formula for unity.

When Jesus prays for unity, he asks his Father that those who believe in him, that is in his full communion with the Father, will become part of that unity. I continue to see in myself and others how often we try to make unity among ourselves by focusing all our attention on each other and trying to find the place where we can feel united. But often we become disillusioned, realizing that no human being is capable of offering us what we most want. Such disillusionment can easily make us become bitter, cynical, demanding, even violent.

Jesus calls us to seek our unity in and through him. When we direct our inner attention not first of all to each other, but to God to whom we belong, then we will discover that in God we also belong to each other. The deepest friendship is a friendship mediated by God; the strongest marriage bonds are bonds mediated by God.

This truth requires the discipline to keep returning to the source of all unity. If, in the midst of conflict, division, and discord, we would always try to enter together in the presence of God to find our unity there, much human suffering could be relieved.

20

One Among Many

Technology and Human Relations

(Cambridge, Mass.; Monday, May 12)

Traveling from Paris to Boston made me sharply aware of the contrast between the great advancements in technology and the primitive quality of human relationships. While the most sophisticated machinery took me from Paris to London in one hour and from London to Boston in six hours, the entire trip was clouded by security concerns. More than an hour before the departure of the flight I had to say good-bye to Nathan and Brad, who were with me at Charles de Gaulle Airport in Paris. They were not allowed to be with me while I was checking in my luggage. In London I had to go through countless security checks and a body search and had to identify the luggage that I had asked to be sent directly to Boston. The delays were connected not with technical concerns, but with security problems.

It is obviously a good thing that so many precautions are being taken to prevent terrorist attacks, but the fact that every step of the way you are made aware that someone might try to kill you gives you a sense that the world is a precarious place to live in. The more advanced the method of transportation, the less safe it seems to be transported! Quite a few of my friends have canceled their vacation plans because of fear of being hijacked, bombed, or attacked on airplanes or in airports.

Technology is so far ahead of human relations! There is such a need for new ways for people to be together, to solve conflicts, to work for peace. On the level of human relations, we are still in the Stone Age, thinking that power games and fear tactics will settle our problems. Suicide attacks and military reprisals are such primitive ways to respond to threatening situations. With the technology now at hand, these primitive responses may cause the end of all human life.

More than ever it is necessary for people, who can fly to each other from faraway distances within a few hours, to speak to each other about living together in peace. Now it seems that the smaller the physical distance, the larger the moral and spiritual distance. Why do we human beings learn so much, so soon, about technology, and so little, so late, about loving one another?

Peter and Jonas welcomed me at Logan International Airport. We were very grateful to be safely together again. Given the violent state of our world, we shouldn't take such reunions for granted.

The Battle for Spiritual Survival

(Tuesday, May 13)

A day filled with joyful reunions. Peter and Kate, Jonas, Marta and Michael, Jutta, David, Jim, and Charles . . . they all came and we talked and prayed together again.

What most strikes me, being back in the United States, is the full force of the restlessness, the loneliness, and the tension that holds so many people. The conversations I had today were about spiritual survival. So many of my friends feel overwhelmed by the many demands made on them; few feel the inner peace and joy they so much desire.

To celebrate life together, to be together in community, to simply enjoy the beauty of creation, the love of people and the goodness of God—those seem faraway ideals. There seems to be a mountain of obstacles preventing people from being where their hearts want to be. It is so painful to watch and experience. The astonishing thing is that the battle for survival has become so "normal" that few people really believe that it can be different. I now understand better why my friends who came to Trosly were so deeply touched. A world they didn't know existed had opened up for them.

The people I saw today are all such good people. They are generous, loving, caring, and filled with a desire for a community of faith; but they all suffer immensely, without always knowing it. Having been away from here for ten months, I can see what I couldn't see when I was in it myself. After having experienced so much spiritual freedom at L'Arche, I am better able to see how much my friends miss. I want so much to bring them to new places, show them new perspectives, and point out to them new ways. But in this hectic, pressured, competitive, exhausting context, who can really hear me? I even wonder how long I myself can stay in touch with the voice of the spirit when the demons of this world make so much noise.

Oh, how important is discipline, community, prayer, silence, caring presence, simple listening, adoration, and deep, lasting, faithful friendship. We all want it so much, and still the powers suggesting that all of that is fantasy are enormous. But we have to replace the battle for power with the battle to create space for the spirit.

Friends of Jesus

(Wednesday, May 14)

The heart of this day was a eucharistic celebration in which about twenty of my Cambridge friends participated. Jesus' words "I shall no longer call you servants, because a servant does not know his master's business; I call you friends, because I have made known to you everything I have learned from my Father" (John 15:15) expressed powerfully the meaning of my reunion with them. We are friends of Jesus not in a sentimental fashion, but as participants in the divine life. If we dare to claim boldly that friendship, then we can also trust in the lasting bond among each other. This mutual friendship is the splendid fruit of our kinship with Jesus. It is much more than an idea. Rather, this friendship is a tangible reality.

Many friends had asked my associate, Peter, if they could come for a short visit; Peter suggested that they all come for a eucharistic celebration, and then lunch. I am convinced that everyone received more than I would have ever been able to give in individual encounters. What I was able to give was the friendship of Jesus expressed in the gifts of bread and wine. At the same time, people from the most different age groups, educational backgrounds, lifestyles, and characters could be together in harmony and peace and discover that their differences actually reveal their deep unity in Christ.

I have been increasingly struck by the fact that the main source of suffering of the people in a city such as Cambridge seems to lie in a sense of disconnectedness, separation, and alienation. Why should I talk with each of them individually about their pain if together they can become a healing community around the table of Christ? It was a truly joyful time in which prayer, songs, and sharing stories revealed the faithful presence of Jesus.

The Poverty of the Rich

(New York; Thursday, May 15)

This morning Peter and I flew to New York City to visit Murray McDonnell. I had never met Murray, but during my time in France, Murray and Peter had come to know each other and had developed a good friendship.

Murray is a New York banker who personally knows countless people I have only heard about on TV or read about in the newspapers. He has read many of my books and feels that his world needs the word of God as much as my world does. It was a very humbling experience to hear a man who knows "the best and the brightest" say, "Give us a word from God, speak to us about Jesus . . . do not stay away from the rich, who are so poor."

Jesus loves the poor—but poverty takes many forms. How easily I forget that fact, leaving the powerful, the famous, and the successful without the spiritual food they crave. But to offer that food, I have to be very poor myself—not curious, not ambitious, not pretentious, not proud. It is so easy to be swept off one's own feet by the glitter of the world, seduced by its apparent splendor. And yet the only place I can really be is the place of poverty, the place where there is loneliness, anger, confusion, depression, and pain. I have to go there in the name of Jesus, staying close to his name and offering his love.

O Lord, help me not to be distracted by power and wealth; help me not to be impressed by knowing the stars and heroes of this world. Open my eyes to the suffering heart of your people, whoever they are, and give me the word that can bring healing and consolation. Amen.

Politicians and Ministry

(Washington, D.C.; Friday, May 16)

Yesterday Peter returned to Boston and I flew on to Washington to visit my friends there. It was a very joyful day, mostly because I was able to stay very close to Jesus during all my conversations and speak simply and directly about him. This was not always easy because of the distraction of so many people and things. Having lunch with Senator Mark Hatfield in the stately quarters of the Senate Appropriations Committee, hearing about the struggle against the fabrication of nerve gas and the attempts to get some solid information about human rights violations in Guatemala, meeting Henry Kissinger in the corridor, and sensing the general atmosphere of busyness and urgency—all of this gave me ample occasion to leave the house of the Lord and roam around curiously searching for power, influence, and success. Yet all day Jesus remained in the center, and the hours were filled with a sense of God's presence.

What most impressed me was the eagerness of all the people I met today to hear about God's presence in this world. It seemed as if I couldn't say enough about it. During my two-hour luncheon with Senator Hatfield and his aides, not a minute was spent talking about politics. All our attention went to questions about the message of the New Testament, living a fruitful life, developing meaningful relationships, prayer, obedience, and faithfulness. As we were talking, I realized that, in fact, we were coming closer to the real problems of the world than a debate on current political issues would have brought us.

At one point in our conversation I asked Senator Hatfield, "How can I be of any help to the U.S. Senate?" He said, "Come and speak to us about forgiveness, reconciliation, and ways to live in peace with each other. So much bitterness and resentment, jealousy and anger exist in the lives of politicians, at work as well as at home, that any healing word will be received with open hands."

Later, Doug Coe asked me to give a retreat to twenty members of the young presidents' organization. I asked him, "Who are the young presidents?" He said, "They are people, mostly men, who have made more than a million dollars before they were thirty years old, who head a company with at least fifty employees, and who have significant influence." I asked, "Why do they want a retreat?" He answered, "They have a great desire to come to know Jesus. They will come to any place in the world, on any day you want, to hear you speak about Jesus."

How much more do I have to know? Why should I want anything but Jesus, where everyone I meet asks me to proclaim him? My only task is to stay in God's house and stop roaming around in the world.

In the midst of all of this, I kept in close touch with Nathan and Jonas. Their prayers and support gave me a sense of safety and protection. I am sent into this world; my friends have to help me not to become part of it.

Being Silent with Friends

(Cambridge, Mass.; Monday, May 19)

Back in Cambridge, the thought keeps coming to me that it is as important to be silent with friends as to speak with them. Seeing so many people and talking with them about all that has happened and is happening to them often leaves me with a sense of not really being together. The exchange of countless details about people's lives can often create more distance than closeness. Words are important in order to come close, but too many words create distance.

I feel an increasing desire to be silent with friends. Not every event has to be told, not every idea has to be exchanged. Once an atmosphere of mutual trust is present, we can be silent together and let the Lord be the one who speaks, gently and softly. Listening together to Jesus is a very powerful way to grow closer to each other and reach a level of intimacy that no interpersonal exchange of words can bring about. A silence lived together in the presence of Jesus will also continue to bear many fruits in the future. It seems as if a caring silence can enter deeper into our memory than many caring words. Maybe not always, but certainly often. But to create this silence requires much spiritual work. It is not the most obvious style for a reunion! And still, it may be the most blessed.

I will try to put this conviction into practice in the days to come.

Welcoming the Child

(Tuesday, May 20)

"Anyone who welcomes a little child such as this in my name, welcomes me; and anyone who welcomes me, welcomes not me but the one who sent me" (Mark 9:37).

What does welcoming a little child mean? It means giving loving attention to those who are often overlooked. I imagine myself standing in line to meet a very important person and noticing a little child passing by. Would I leave the line and pay all my attention to this child? I imagine myself going to a grand party where I will meet very interesting and powerful people. Could I forget about the party to sit on the street for a few hours with a man who stretches out his hands and asks me for some money? I imagine myself being invited to receive an award. Could I let the honor go to spend the time with a depressed, elderly woman who is forgotten by her friends and feels isolated in her apartment?

Yesterday I was stopped on the street by a beggar. He asked me for some change to buy a bite to eat. He didn't expect any response, but when I gave him ten dollars he jumped up and said,

"Thank you, thank you very, very much." He was extremely surprised by this large gift, but I suddenly felt a deep sadness. I was on my way to a meeting I did not want to miss. My gift was an excuse for walking on. I had not welcomed the beggar—I had just tried to feel generous. My "generosity" had revealed my deep resistance toward welcoming the "little child."

To welcome the "little child" I have to become little myself. But I continue to wonder how great I am. Even my generosity can help me to feel great. But Jesus said, "If anyone wants to be first, he must make himself last of all and servant of all" (Mark 9:35). Am I willing to become the servant of this beggar? By giving him ten dollars I became his master, who could make him say, "Thank you, thank you very much."

It is becoming clear to me that I still have not understood that Jesus revealed his love to us by becoming our servant, and calls us to follow him in this way.

21

A Hard but Blessed Vocation

**Thinking Together
About the Future**

(Toronto; Friday, May 23)

Early this morning I flew to Toronto, where Sue Mosteller welcomed me and drove me to Daybreak in Richmond Hill.

I have been looking forward to my days at Daybreak because it is going to be my home for at least three years. I now feel that my year at Trosly is coming to an end and that I am getting ready to accept a new responsibility. During the past few months so many different things have been happening in my life that I have hardly had the time or energy to think about my future life and work at Daybreak; but now that seems the only important thing.

At 2:30 P.M. the Daybreak council invited me to tell them about my own spiritual journey and reasons for accepting their call to come to Canada and be their pastor. After having tried to express to them as best I could my own sense of being called away from Harvard and being called to a life with handicapped people and their assistants, they told me about the way they had been thinking about my future presence at Daybreak.

Five aspects arose: (1) I have a lot to learn. I have never really lived in community or close to handicapped people. It will not be easy to enter into this small world after having moved around so much in the big world. Therefore, I will need a good period to become a true part of the life here. (2) Together we need to develop a rich spiritual life that allows us to celebrate the liturgical year, broaden our knowledge of the scriptures, and deepen our prayer life. (3) One of my main tasks will be to help start "The Dayspring," a small spiritual center that can be a source of renewal for English-speaking L'Arche members and their friends. (4) I should continue writing. This will not be easy, since there are so many things that will compete for my attention. But the community will not only honor, but also protect and support my vocation to write. (5) Then there will be the letters, the phone calls, the speaking engagements, and so on. It is a blessing to know that Connie Ellis is available to assist me in this work.

As we talked, I had the distinct feeling that it will not be easy to be here, but also that I will not be alone in my struggle. I thought, "It is going to be hard but blessed. I am called to this place of weak and broken people. It is a call coming from God and God's people. Do not worry, just move into it and trust that you will find what your heart most desires." Daybreak is not a place of power. It is not a smooth operation in which efficiency and control are priorities. On the contrary, it is a fellowship of the weak, in which nothing is fully together and everything has a somewhat tentative quality. I can see how frustrating this can be for me, considering my desire to get things done, and done quickly. But I trust that the slow and inefficient way of life at Daybreak will teach me something new about God's love that has remained unknown to me so far.

The Way to a
Second Childhood

(Saturday, May 24)

This morning I wondered what the Gospel reading would be. Often I have the feeling that the Gospel of the day will tell me all I have to know.

I read, "Let the little children come to me; do not stop them; for it is to such as these that the kingdom of God belongs. In truth I tell you, anyone who does not welcome the kingdom of God like a little child will never enter it" (Mark 10:14–15).

What is so special about a little child? The little child has nothing to prove, nothing to show, nothing to be proud of. All the child needs to do is to receive the love that is offered. Jesus wants us to receive the love he offers. He wants nothing more than that we allow him to love us and enjoy that love. This is so hard since we always feel that we have to deserve the love offered to us. But Jesus wants to offer that love to us not because we have earned it, but because he has decided to love us independently of any effort on our side. Our own love for each other should flow from that "first love" that is given to us undeserved.

As I was reflecting on Jesus' words, I started to see more clearly how Daybreak could help me not only to receive the little children, but also to become like one of them. The handicapped may be able to show me the way to a second childhood. Indeed, they can reveal to me God's first love. Handicapped people have little, if anything, to show to the world. They have no degrees, no reputation, no influence, no connections with influential people; they do not create much, produce much, or earn much. They have to trust that they can receive and give pure love. I have already received so many hugs and kisses here from people who have never heard of me and are not the least impressed by me that I have to start believing that the love they offer is freely given, to be freely received.

My dream is that Daybreak can increasingly become a place where the first love of God is revealed to people anxious to prove they deserve love. A house of prayer and welcome, in which handicapped people could receive guests searching for God, might be a concrete way to exercise the ministry of that first love.

During the meeting of the Daybreak board today, I expressed some of these thoughts. The members—lawyers, doctors, and businessmen—were very open and very receptive. They themselves had come to know within their busy lives that they, too, need to hear that still small voice saying, "I love you whether you are important or not, whether you are a failure or not, whether you have money or not, whether you are handsome or not." They had joined the board of this unpretentious community because they wanted to stay in touch with that voice.

A New Family

(Sunday, May 25)

A new family! I have been invited to make the "New House" my home. It is the home of Raymond, John, Bill, Trevor, Adam, Rose, and their three assistants, D.J., Heather, and Regina. I am staying with them for this short visit, but it appears as if I will live here when I return in August and make this my permanent home. It is a remarkable family. Rose and Adam are deeply handicapped and need constant attention and care. They cannot speak or walk, feed or dress themselves; they live in a world seemingly impenetrable. They need to be dressed, washed, fed, and carried. Only when they sleep can they be alone.

Raymond, John, Bill, and Trevor are quite independent compared with Rose and Adam. They speak a lot, go to workshops during the day, and can help with small tasks in the house.

It was a special joy to see Raymond again. He was completely recovered from his October accident and looked better than before. He didn't remember me at all, but his parents had told him so much about me that he received me with special kindness. We soon became friends and spent quite a bit of time together.

D.J., the house leader, is a very caring twenty-four-year-old Canadian who gives all his time and energy to his Daybreak family. Heather, from Omaha, Nebraska, is finishing her year in the house and will return to her family within a few months. Regina came from Brazil and will soon be joined by her sister.

Living in community is not going to be easy for me. But after two days with this family, I already feel a desire to come back and get to know them all more intimately. That is all that counts for the moment.

22

Contrasts and Choices

On the Balcony

(Berkeley, Calif.; Tuesday, May 27)

After a meeting with the assistants of Daybreak, we celebrated a quiet and prayerful Eucharist together. Soon after the conclusion of the Eucharist, Sue Mosteller drove me to the Toronto airport, where I caught a plane to San Francisco to visit my friend Don McNeill.

Don is a Holy Cross priest and director of the Center for Social Concerns at the University of Notre Dame. We have been close friends since 1966, when I went to Notre Dame as a visiting professor. Last year Don was suddenly hit by brachial plexus neuropathy, a muscular disease that has seriously affected his physical movements. Doctors expect that he will need at least two years before he will regain his full strength. Don himself has some real doubts about whether he will ever again be the agile, fast-moving man he was before the disease hit him. Presently he is spending a year at one of the Holy Cross houses in Berkeley to have the rest and space needed for his recovery. I decided to spend a few days with him, to offer him some courage and confidence in this trying time in his life and to celebrate the twentieth anniversary of our friendship.

We are now sitting on the balcony of the Holy Cross house in Berkeley. It must be one of the most beautiful spots in the world. I am looking out over San Francisco Bay. In the far distance I recognize the lighthouse of Alcatraz Island, and behind it the outline of the Golden Gate Bridge. As the darkness slowly covers the bay area, the view is gradually transformed by a myriad of lights telling me of all the different people living around the water. It is very quiet on the balcony—the city is too far away to hear its sounds. The air is gentle and warm, full of scents coming from the blooming trees.

After the busy day at Daybreak and the long, tiring flight, sitting quietly with my friend on this balcony overlooking the wide waters and the city aglow with lights, I marvel at being alive and being able to be part of it all.

The Senses and the Spirit

(Wednesday, May 28)

Being in California is exciting as well as disturbing to me. It is very hard for me to describe the emotions this world calls forth in me. The pleasant climate, the lush gardens, the splendid trees and flowerbeds, the beautiful view over the bay, the city, the island, and the bridges call forth in me words of praise, gratitude, and joy. But the countless car lots, the intense traffic, the huge advertisements, the new buildings going up all over the place, the smog, the noises, the fastness of living—all of this makes me feel unconnected, lonely, and a little lost.

Maybe the word that summarizes it all is "sensual." All my senses are being stimulated, but with very little grounding, very little history, very little spirit. I keep wondering how my heart can be fed in this world. It seems as if everyone is moving quickly to meet some person or go to some place or some event. But nobody has much of a home. The houses look very temporary. They will probably last a few decades, maybe a century, but then something else will take their place.

The people we meet are very friendly, easygoing, casual, and entertaining; but I keep wondering how to be with them, how to speak with them, how to pray with them. Everything is very open, expressive, and new; but I find myself looking for a space that is hidden, silent, and old. This is a land to which people go in order to be free from tradition, constraints, and an oppressive history. But the price for this freedom is high: individualism, competition, rootlessness, and frequently loneliness and a sense of being lost. When anything goes, everything is allowed, everything is worth a try, then nothing is sacred, nothing venerable, nothing worth much respect. Being young, daring, original, and mobile seems to be the ideal. Old things need to be replaced by new things, and old people are to be pitied.

The body is central. The sun, the beaches, the water, and the lushness of nature open up all the senses. But it is hard to experience the body as the temple of the spirit. That requires a very special discipline. To reach that inner sanctum where God's voice can be heard and obeyed is not easy if you are always called outward. It is not surprising that California has become a place where many spiritual disciplines are being discovered, studied, and practiced. There are many meditation centers—Buddhist, Christian, and nonreligious. More and more people feel a need to discover an inner anchor to keep themselves whole in the midst of the sensual world.

So here I am, somewhat overwhelmed by it all and somewhat confused. How am I to be faithful to Jesus in a world in which having a body is celebrated in so many ways? Jesus is the God who became flesh with us so that we could live with his spirit. How do I live out this truth in this sun-covered, sensual, nontraditional place? Maybe I wouldn't even have raised this question had L'Arche not opened my eyes to a completely different way of thinking about the body. At L'Arche, too, the body is central, but what a difference!

I am glad to be with Don, who is suffering so much in his body, and to share with him Jean's vision that the community of L'Arche is formed around the wounded bodies of handicapped people. I realize that Don and I are bound together by twenty years of friendship, a friendship that seems so very long and solid when set against this transitory milieu.

Death in the Castro District

(San Francisco; Saturday, May 31)

Don dropped me off in the Castro district of San Francisco to visit a friend who had recently moved there. It is hard to find words to describe this glittering gay district of San Francisco.

If ever the word "gay" seemed a euphemism, it is in today's Castro, where many young men die of AIDS every day and thousands more worry that they are carrying the virus that causes the disease. As my friend and I walked through the busy streets to find a restaurant, I thought of John. A few years ago he showed me the district and told me all about the life there. Then the word "AIDS" was hardly known. Now John is dead after a long, devastating illness, and many have shared his agony. Behind a facade of opulent wealth, a great variety of entertainment, large stores with posters, printed T-shirts, greeting cards, and all sorts of playful knickknacks lies an immense fear. And not only fear but also guilt, feelings of rejection, anger, fatalism, careless hedonism, and, in the midst of it all, trust, hope, love, and the rediscovery of God in the face of death.

As I walked with my friend on the streets of the Castro district, we saw countless men walking up and down the sidewalks just looking at each other, gazing into store windows, standing on corners in small groups, and going in and out of bars, theaters, video shops, drugstores, and restaurants. It seemed as if everyone was waiting for something that would bring them a sense of being deeply loved, fully accepted, and truly at home. But evident in the eyes of many was deep suffering, anguish, and loneliness, because what they most seek and most desire seems most elusive. Many have not been able to find a lasting home or a safe relationship, and now, with the AIDS threat, fear has become all-pervasive.

And yet AIDS has unleashed not only fear, but also an enormous generosity. Many people are showing great care for each other, great courage in helping each other, great faithfulness, and often unwavering love. I sensed an enormous need for God's love to be made known to these fearful and often generous people. More than ever the Church has to live out Christ's love for the poor, the sinners, the publicans, the rejected, the possessed, and all who desperately need to be loved. As I saw the countless gay men on the streets, I kept thinking about the great consolation that Jesus came to offer. He revealed the total and unlimited love of God for humanity. This is the love that the Church is called to make visible not by judging, condemning, or segregating, but by serving everyone in need. I often wonder if the many heated debates about the morality of homosexuality do not prevent the Christian community from reaching out fearlessly to its suffering fellow humans.

Happily, many encouraging new initiatives are being taken. On February 2, Archbishop Roger Mahony published a pastoral letter in which he took concrete steps to assist the victims of AIDS and offered important guidelines for the overall pastoral care of gay Catholic men and women. He called for the establishment of a hospice for AIDS victims and for the formation of gay Catholic groups that would help their members to live chaste lives "according to the will of the Father as manifested in the Scriptures and the official teachings of the Roman Catholic Church."

My friend and I talked much about Jesus, and as I left he said, "I am glad you came. There are too few people who mention his name in the district. There are so many negative associations with his name, and still he is the greatest source of hope."

The Body of Christ

(Sunday, June 1)

Today is the feast of Corpus Christi, the body of Christ. As Edward Malloy, a visiting Holy Cross priest, Don, and I celebrated the Eucharist in the little Chapel of the Holy Cross house in Berkeley, the importance of this feast touched me more than ever. The illness that has severely impaired Don's movements made him, and also me, very conscious of the beauty, intricacy, and fragility of the human body. My visit yesterday to the Castro district, where physical pleasure is so visibly sought and bodily pain so dramatically suffered, reminded me powerfully that I not only *have* a body, but also *am* a body. The way one lives in the body, the way one relates to, cares for, exercises, and uses one's own and other people's bodies, is of crucial importance for one's spiritual life.

The greatest mystery of the Christian faith is that God came to us in the body, suffered with us in the body, rose in the body, and gave us his body as food. No religion takes the body as seriously as the Christian religion. The body is not seen as the enemy or as a prison of the spirit, but celebrated as the spirit's temple. Through Jesus' birth, life, death, and resurrection, the human body has become part of the life of God. By eating the body of Christ, our own fragile bodies are becoming intimately connected with the risen Christ and thus prepared to be lifted up with him into the divine life. Jesus says, "I am the living bread which has come down from heaven. Anyone who eats this bread will live forever; and the bread that I shall give is my flesh, for the life of the world" (John 6:51).

It is in union with the body of Christ that I come to know the full significance of my own body. My body is much more than a mortal instrument of pleasure and pain. It is a home where God wants to manifest the fullness of the divine glory. This truth is the

most profound basis for the moral life. The abuse of the body—
whether it be psychological (e.g., instilling fear), physical (e.g.,
torture), economic (e.g., exploitation), or sexual (e.g., hedonistic
pleasure seeking)—is a distortion of true human destiny: to live in
the body eternally with God. The loving care given to our bodies
and the bodies of others is therefore a truly spiritual act, since it
leads the body closer toward its glorious existence.

I wonder how I can bring this good news to the many people
for whom their body is little more than an unlimited source of
pleasure or an unceasing source of pain. The feast of the body of
Christ is given to us to fully recognize the mystery of the body and
to help us find ways to live reverently and joyfully in the body in
expectation of the risen life with God.

Expensive
Sandbox Games

(Los Angeles; Monday, June 2)

Yesterday, Don and I said our good-byes and I flew to Los Angeles
to spend a day with my friends Chris Glaser and Richard White
before moving back eastward.

My friendship with Chris dates from the years that I taught at
Yale Divinity School. For several years he worked as a lay minister
at the West Hollywood Presbyterian Church, and presently he
dedicates all of his time to writing. It was good to see Chris at the
airport and to hear him speak with enthusiasm about the last
phases of his book *Uncommon Calling: A Gay Man's Struggle to
Serve the Church*, a book full of pain, full of struggle, but also full of
hope. Chris is a man of great faith who has never allowed bitterness to conquer gratitude. During his many years in the ministry,
Chris has shared many of his struggles with me, and his current
book is a public testimony of his faithful search to integrate his
sexuality with his faith.

Together with Chris's friend George Lynch, we had a very nice dinner in a quiet West Hollywood restaurant and ample opportunity to share what we had been living during the past few years.

This morning Chris drove me to the house where Richard White is staying. Richard and I have been friends since 1966, when we met in Cuernavaca, Mexico. Our common interest in Latin America brought us together and was the beginning of a friendship that—though stormy at times—has always grown deeper and stronger. This time, unexpectedly, Richard gave me a fascinating glimpse into the filmmaking industry.

I stayed in the house of Richard's friend Jack, a Los Angeles film producer. For four months he had been out of work, and his financial situation had become so critical that he was thinking about subletting parts of his house to get enough money to pay his bills. But last week everything changed. He was hired to become the producer of an NBC situation comedy called "Amen," which will be broadcast this coming fall. Suddenly Jack has a splendid office with a large staff and a salary of $2,700 a week! If the series proves to be successful, his salary will substantially increase, and if he establishes himself as a sought-after producer, he will be a millionaire within a few years. If things fail, he will be subletting his house soon because he likes to spend money as much as to earn it.

The "Amen" series revolves around the shenanegans of an outrageous deacon who manipulates his all-black church and its congregation. Although its scripts include some social and ethical issues, it is still very much the standard formula TV network sitcom.

My friend Richard White, who has been staying with Jack for the past few months, called Jack's work "sandbox games." Jack totally agreed—he was playing with a two-million-dollar project, the purpose of which was to make a lot of money by giving a couple of million viewers some good laughs.

As Jack was talking to me, full of excitement about his new job and all the money he was going to make, I was struck by the blatant superficiality of it all. Jack himself is a paradox of our culture. He reads Jean-Paul Sartre, is trying to find funding for an excellent movie script he wrote on one man's courageous stand against the Nazis, and is working on another script about apartheid in South Africa. At the same time he calls himself a "hired gun," eager to sell his talents to the Hollywood production companies. Like many cinemagraphic artists, he sees the world through the eyes of the camera and is enthralled with the visual effects his art can create almost without regard for the subject matter.

As Richard and I had dinner, Richard asked me, "Why do the people who want to stop war, prevent torture, make people aware of injustice, and care for the sick and the handicapped never have enough money, while those who play these sandbox games earn more than they know what to do with?"

It is the question that haunted the Old Testament prophets and psalmists and is still haunting us today. I could only say, "Let us not be jealous. God loves the poor and the humble of heart. That knowledge should be enough." But the fact that I was not wholly without jealousy and resentment showed that maybe God was not as real for me as the sandbox games are for Jack.

A Vision and a Task

(London; Wednesday, June 11)

On my way from California to Paris I am spending a few days in London. This afternoon I visited Donald Reeves, the pastor of St. James's Anglican Church in Piccadilly.

Donald Reeves is a man of many gifts: He is an activist, a contemplative, a social worker, an artist, a caring pastor, a restless mover, a visionary, and a pragmatist. In five years he converted a practically lifeless downtown Anglican parish into a vibrant center of prayer and action. When I arrived at the rectory I could sense the vibrancy of the place: Within a few minutes I had met a bishop, a Jew, an ex-convict, an artist, and an administrator. Donald introduced them all to me with words of praise and encouragement. You could sense that people were doing new things here, things they believed in. The parish is a place for meditation, counseling, art events, concerts, peacemaking, book publishing, and hospitality. It is a place that welcomes traditional Christians as well as people who feel alienated from the Church. It is an incredibly diverse place, embracing charismatics as well as activists, Christians as well as non-Christians.

Listening to Donald, I realized how much he had been influenced by new communities in the United States, especially the Sojourners' Fellowship and the Church of the Savior in Washington, D.C. I felt invigorated just being with him and walking around the place with him. I was ready to promise all sorts of things: lectures, retreats, writing, conversations, and discussions. But I controlled my impulse to help and asked for simple fellowship instead. Being connected with this church as a friend, a supporter, and a fellow traveler seems most important of all.

As I left, Donald gave me some of his writings. On the cover of his "ten-year plan" for the Church he wrote:

A vision without a task is a dream;
A task without a vision is drudgery;
A vision and a task is the hope of the world.

Nothing better can sum up the spirit of St. James's of Piccadilly than these words.

Filmmaking for Peace

(Thursday, June 12)

I spent the whole day with Bart Gavigan and Patricia Beall. They first came to see me in Cambridge in May 1985, while they were preparing a film about George Zabelka, the Air Force chaplain turned pacifist. Although we had met for only a few hours, we had experienced a deep bond among us and a sense that Jesus had brought us together to support each other in our spiritual journeys. Seldom have I felt so strongly that friendship is a gift of God, not the result of long hours of conversation, shared activities, and deep knowledge of each other's lives. It was simply there—suddenly, directly, unprepared-for. We stayed in touch by letter, and when we saw each other again last night it felt as if we had known each other for a long time and were part of a God-given union.

During the morning we spoke about our lives, not so much to get to know each other as to be witnesses to each other of the marvelous ways in which God has touched our hearts.

After celebrating the Eucharist together in the parish church and having a meal in a London restaurant, we went to the Soho district, where Bart had rented a studio to cut *The Reluctant Prophet,* the film about George Zabelka that is now in its final stage of editing. It was quite an experience for me. We walked through the crowded district full of market stalls, porno shops, and shouting people. In the middle of all this craziness, we found Bart's little cutting room. Then we sat watching the beginning of a gripping documentary about the priest who after having blessed those who dropped the atomic bomb on Hiroshima, was converted to a committed peacemaker. It struck me that we were sitting in a dark upstairs studio watching a film about peacemaking while voices of lust and violence surrounded us on all sides.

Bart is a very unusual filmmaker. When he discovered that in most filmmaking the communication of ideas and ideals is completely subservient to the making of profits, he joined a Christian community to test his priorities. Now, many years later, he is ready to make films not for money, but to follow Jesus' way. In this lustful and violent world he has to risk his money and reputation to do what he feels called to do, but he is determined to do what is just and right, and he trusts that the rest will be given to him. For Bart, filmmaking is ministry.

I never dreamed that I would meet within a few days a filmmaker so different from the one I met in Los Angeles. What Jack is doing in the splendid offices of Johnny Carson Productions and what Bart is doing in his upstairs cutting room in Soho is the same work of filmmaking. But they reveal two completely different worlds. I keep being struck by the importance of making choices.

Evaluating a Journey

(Paris; Monday, June 23)

When I arrived in Paris, Brad Wolcott was waiting for me. Together we went to the Foyer Sacerdotal, a hostel for priests in Paris where Brad had reserved a room for me.

So here I am back in Paris. The bright evening sun made the city look festive and welcoming. Brad called it the "New Jerusalem." During supper I tried to express my feelings about the journey that had started on May 12. As I spoke, I became more and more conscious of the ups and downs of my inner journey that had gone on while I traveled the world. It had become possible for me to identify clearly when I had been faithful and when not. There were days in which I felt very much connected with Jesus—thinking, speaking, and acting in communion with him. But there were also days when I felt so needy, distant, anxious, or restless that Jesus seemed far away. There were days during which I could speak loudly and clearly about the love of God and was listened to with great attention. But there were other days when I seemed to have lost even my inner spiritual life and looked with jealous eyes at those who enjoyed the good life without even the slightest thought of God.

It is important that I know the difference between these two states of mind and can identify when and how I move from one to the other. The most important criterion is prayer. As long as I pray daily, intimately and long, I stay in the right place and continue to walk on the road to faithfulness. But when I let my prayer go because of fatigue, distraction, or laziness, I know that I will soon be on the other side of the fence. The second criterion is a deep, confessing friendship. I now realize that I need regular contact with a friend who keeps me close to Jesus and continues to call me to faithfulness.

As I talked to Brad, I realized that I had come to know my limits better and to realize more clearly how to deal with them.

True Belonging

(Tuesday, June 24)

Being back in France makes me think much about countries and cultures. During the past few months I have been in Holland, Germany, Canada, the United States, and England, and in all these countries I have had intense contact with people and their ways of living, praying, and playing.

There is a great temptation to want to know which culture is the best and where I am most happy and at home. But this way of thinking leads to endless frustrations because the Dutch, the Germans, the French, the Americans, and the Canadians are all people who have unique ways of feeling, thinking, and behaving, none of which totally fits my needs, but all of which have gifts for me.

I know people who complain about the Germans while in Germany and about the Americans while in America, moving themselves and their families back and forth, always wondering what the best place is to live without ever being truly content. Some people, then, are always disappointed with someone or something. They complain about the rigidity of the German Church and the sloppiness of the American Church. Or they may complain about the critical attitude of the Dutch, the mystical attitude of the French, the pragmatic attitude of the Americans, and the formalistic attitude of the English, while never really worshiping deeply at any one place.

I am increasingly aware of how important it is to enjoy what is given and to fully live where one is. If I could just fully appreciate the need for independence of the Dutch, the spiritual visions of the French, the concreteness of the Americans, the theological concepts of the Germans, and the sense of ceremony of the English, I could come to learn much about life everywhere and truly become present to where I am, always growing deeper in the spirit of gratitude.

Do we really need to belong to one country or one culture? In our world, where distances are becoming less each day, it seems important to become less and less dependent on one place, one language, one culture, or one style of life, but to experience oneself as a member of the human family, belonging to God and free to be wherever we are called to be. I even wonder if the ability to be in so many places so quickly and so often is not an invitation to grow deeper in the spirit and let our identity be more rooted in God and less in the place in which we happen to be.

23

Endings and Beginnings

Questions About Faithfulness

(Trosly; Wednesday, June 25)

Last night I returned to Trosly; it was a mixed experience to be back. On the one hand, it felt like coming home after six weeks of traveling. On the other hand, it made me aware that Trosly had not become a true home for me. I had remained too much on the periphery of the life here. People said "Hello" and "Welcome back," but it was clear that I had remained a stranger who lives his own life and does his own things.

Nathan was so busy in his foyer that we had to wait until this afternoon to see each other. I was so eager to reconnect with him and feel welcomed back by him that the delay was painful and frustrating. But when he could finally leave his work and come to my room, we had a blessed time together. It was like a spiritual debriefing.

The question "How was the trip?" was not a question about events and people, but a question about faithfulness to God amidst all the events and people, faithfulness in thoughts, words, and deeds. It was good for me to "confess" to Nathan my many ups and downs in the struggle to remain anchored in Jesus. As I looked at my journey in the perspective of this struggle, I found much to confess, much to be grateful for, but also much to feel repentant about. It is so important to be specific and concrete and to identify accurately the moments of faithfulness and unfaithfulness, as generalities do not help much in the spiritual life. Specifics are crucial —they tell the real story. They reveal the real sin and the real grace; they point the real way to renewal.

After this "confession" to Nathan, I felt more at home again and more connected. I will only be here for two more weeks. I hope I can live these weeks in a faithful and prayerful way.

Spiritual Fatigue

(Friday, June 27)

My long journey has harmed my prayer life. I have discovered how hard it has become for me to spend one hour in the morning simply being present to Jesus. I experience a certain nausea or apathy that I did not have before I left. It is a sort of spiritual fatigue, a state of lukewarmness in which I find it hard to know exactly what I feel, what I think, or what I want. It is like being a piece of driftwood on still water. Nothing seems to move, and there seems to be no way to get things moving again. I am tired, but I do not sleep well. I am talking to people, but I do not feel well connected. I do many things, but not much is happening. I do not feel depressed, just empty and somewhat indifferent. Maybe it is a temporary "burnout." Well, I am not panicky about it and try to stay in touch with Jesus. What helps me most is praying with others. I very much enjoy saying my morning and evening prayers with friends, and I am very grateful when Nathan prays with me. Friends keep me close to Jesus. I just have to drink in their love and let them pray with and for me.

Peter and Paul

(Sunday, June 29)

Today is the feast of Sts. Peter and Paul. I have often wondered why these two great apostles are celebrated on the same day. Is not each of them worth a special day?

In his sermon, Père Thomas responded to this question. He explained how there is always a danger of playing out one against the other: Peter, the simple, uneducated fisherman who had hardly any knowledge of the theological debates of his time and who responded to Jesus in a direct, impulsive way without much distance or criticism; and Paul, the well-educated disciple of Gamaliel, a Pharisee, sharp, intelligent, deeply concerned about the truth, and willing to persecute those whom he considered in grave error. The Church is built on the foundations laid by both Peter and Paul. There are not two churches, one for the simple people who trust their emotions more than their brains and the other for the intellectuals who are willing to debate the current issues. There is only one church, in which Peter and Paul each has his own role and importance. Uncritical Christianity is as dangerous as "pure brain" Christianity. And indeed Paul had deep emotions and Peter engaged in fierce debates. Within the Church there will always be people who romanticize Peter or intellectualize Paul. It is important that both stay together, not only on their feast day, but also in our own way of living a faithful life.

Trusting the First Love

(Tuesday, July 1)

Tonight I celebrated my last Tuesday Mass for the English-speaking people in the community. Quite a few visitors came, and there was a spirit of quiet, joyful celebration.

Coming "home" to Trosly has not been easy for me. After the long trip, I felt a need to be truly welcomed back. But with so many people coming and going, the permanent members of the community often cannot pay attention to everyone's needs. What I have learned is that God's unlimited love often expresses itself through the limited love of God's people. This means concretely that we broken, sinful people need to confess and forgive day in and day out, and thus continue to reveal a love that we ourselves cannot make true. Over and over again we experience moments of disappointment and disillusionment which can lead to resentment and feelings of anger unless we keep confessing our unfulfilled needs and forgiving each other for not being God for each other. Thus, a community in which confession and forgiveness is a way of life keeps us close to Jesus, who calls us together to make his divine love known.

Today's celebration became an occasion for me to express my own struggles and help others recognize their own. As I looked around the circle, I realized that this small congregation contained representatives from at least six different countries. We knew each other only superficially, but around the word of Christ and his body and blood we became an intimate community of people able to express to each other the unlimited and unconditional love, the "first love" of God. I marveled at this mystery, and I started to feel its healing effect in my heart.

In a Prison Without Walls

(Thursday, July 3)

A very intense day. Many people came by for the Sacrament of Reconciliation or just to talk about their pains and fears. As I listened to their feelings of loneliness, rejection, guilt, and shame, I became overwhelmed by the sense of isolation we human beings can feel. While our sufferings are so similar and our struggles so much a part of our shared humanity, we often live as if we are the only ones who experience the pain that paralyzes us! At one point during the day I felt a desire to bring together all those who had spoken to me this day. I wanted to ask them to share their stories with one another so that they could discover how much they had in common and in this way become a source of consolation and comfort to each other.

Why do we keep hiding our deepest feelings from each other? We suffer much, but we also have great gifts of healing for each other. The mystery is that by hiding our pain we also hide our ability to heal. Even in such a loving and caring community as this, there is more loneliness than necessary. We are called to confess to each other and forgive each other, and thus to discover the abundant mercy of God. But at the same time, we are so terribly afraid of being hurt more than we already are. This fear keeps us prisoners, even when the prison has no walls! I see better every day how radical Jesus' message of love really is.

A Year Full of Graces

(Sunday, July 6)

A day of farewell. My year in Trosly is coming to an end. On Tuesday I am going to Belgium to visit Cardinal Daneels, on Wednesday and Thursday I will be in Holland to say good-bye to my father, brothers, and sister, and on Friday I will be on my way back to Boston.

During the past few days I have been trying to evaluate my time at L'Arche. Was it worth it? I didn't write as much as I had planned; I didn't pray as much as I had hoped; I didn't learn French as well as I had desired; and I didn't come to know the handicapped people as intimately as I had wanted. And still the year has been full of graces.

The first grace was getting back in touch with Europe. Spending time in France, Germany, Belgium, Holland, and England has helped me to feel strongly connected with my roots and to understand in more depth the spiritual tradition of which I am a part. I feel as if I have come into closer touch with the great movement of the spirit of God that has shaped the hearts and minds of many of my European contemporaries, and I have come to trust their spiritual institutions as the main source of my own ministry.

The second grace is friends. If there is any name I would like to give this year, it is "the year of friendships." Much of my time has been dedicated to making new friends and deepening old friendships. Sometimes I felt guilty about spending so little time doing things and so much time "just talking." But now I know that many of the bonds that have been formed have created a mysterious network of affection that will allow me not only to speak with new vigor about God's first love, but also to act more simply, directly, and unambiguously in the service of Jesus, whose mission was to reveal that first love to us. The many old friends who came here from the United States and discovered L'Arche with me, and the many new friends who were given to me, have truly showed me that God became flesh and that the divine love becomes tangible in the affection of God's people.

I will never think about this year without a deep gratitude for my friendship with Nathan and our long hours of sharing our joys and pains. Often it seems to me that the main reason for my being in Trosly was to be given this friendship as the safe context for a new vocation. Whatever happens at Daybreak, I am not going to be alone in my struggle, and Nathan will be there with me to keep me faithful to my promises.

I will also never think about the year without thinking about the friendship of Jean Vanier, Madame Vanier, Simone, Barbara, Thérèse-Monique, Jean-Louis, and the Peeters family. This afternoon Jean-Louis invited all of us to his foyer, La Vigne, where I celebrated the Eucharist. A reception followed with kind words and a joyful dinner. As I felt overwhelmed by the affection shown to me, I tried to receive it as an expression of God's generous love and an affirmation of being called to L'Arche.

The third grace is the beginning of a deeper contact with handicapped people. When I saw Gérard and Michelle of Le Surgeon and all the men of La Vigne at the Eucharist and sensed their presence, a deep gratitude welled up in me and I knew that a new knowledge had been given to me, the knowledge of God that comes from the poor. Gérard's silent smile and the simple way he reached out from his wheelchair to touch my cheek told me things that no words can say. Gérard will never be able to express his inner life in words and will never be able to say, "I love you," and yet he still says something about God's unconditional love that only he can say. Michelle, as always, pointed with her spastic fingers to her own cheeks to be sure that I give her at least two kisses, and the men of La Vigne had their own—often funny— ways of making me feel welcome.

I know that the world of handicapped people is still rather unknown to me. During this past year I did not live in a foyer and remained somewhat an outsider. Still, the year has helped me to make my first steps into this new world, and it has opened in me the hope of a more committed life at Daybreak. I am grateful for all that this year has given to me, and I pray that I can remember it all as a source of hope during difficult times.

Where Sadness and Joy Become One

(Tuesday, July 8)

At 7 P.M. I celebrated the Eucharist in Madame Vanier's living room. Madame Vanier sat in her great chair. Around her were Barbara, Simone, Nathan, Christine, Jean-Louis, Jeff, and Micha.

After the Eucharist Jean-Louis embraced me for a long time and let his tears flow freely. I felt immensely grateful. His abundant tears were the greatest gift he could have given me. Except for my mother, I had never seen anyone cry for me. Jean-Louis simply cried for me. He wore the cap and scarf I had given him on Sunday. As I looked into his eyes and held him in my arms, I felt a communion that cut to the heart. I felt both sadness and joy; two friends were deeply feeling the pain and joy of friendship.

I gave Madame Vanier my chalice and communion plate with the lectionary and the sacramentary. I wanted her to feel that while something was coming to an end, something would also endure.

I was first welcomed to Les Marronniers by Madame Vanier only eleven months ago. We have celebrated the Eucharist together in her living room many times since then. A bond has grown, a bond that will last, a bond, too, that makes this farewell very hard. But the fact that I was going to Canada, her home country, and was joining the Daybreak community, where she has so many friends, eased the pain a little. "It won't be easy there. It won't be easy," she kept saying, "but you will do all right." I was glad that leaving was, in fact, going to the place she most wanted me to go to. As we embraced, I felt deep gratitude for the home she made for me and great joy that in that home I had heard so clearly the call of Jesus to follow him to a new place.

by emerging feelings of tenderness and care. I even began to miss him when I was away for a few days, and when home I came to enjoy just sitting with him, rubbing noses, caressing his face, or playing with his fingers. Thus a stranger became a friend. Friendships also developed with the other handicapped members of the house. Bill started to give me hugs and John to take me out for a beer. Trevor began to give me flowers and Raymond to show me the new ways he had decorated his room. And even Rose, who is profoundly handicapped like Adam, volunteered some really beautiful smiles. It was not always easy to feel at home with these wounded people because there is so much pain and rejection hiding underneath the hugs, the beers, the flowers, and the smiles, but what they give is so freely given that it creates deep affective bonds.

But these bonds did not develop without great cost. It was the cost of facing my own handicaps! I had always known they were there, but I had always been able to keep them out of sight. But those who cannot hide their handicaps do not allow the assistants to hide theirs either. The director of the community and some of the long-term members, as well as the assistants in the house, offered me much support and guidance during my first months. They knew from their own experience that a life with handicapped people involves a radical self-confrontation, and they showed remarkable patience and care as I lived through my own fears and insecurities. Once I said to them, "I first thought I came to help you care for handicapped people, but now I feel as if you had accepted one more handicapped person among you." Indeed, the facing of my own handicaps was the hardest battle of all.

First of all, I had to come to terms with the fact that I had not lived a family life since I was eighteen years old, and here I was faced with a large house to be cleaned, big meals to be cooked, countless dishes to be washed, and stacks of laundry to be done, not to mention shopping, doctors' appointments, bookkeeping, transportation, and the never-ending need for repairs. After thirty-seven years of living in schools where all these things were taken care of, family life made me aware of my lack of the most ordinary skills. Making a dinner for eleven people filled me with great fear and, except for sunny-side-up eggs, every request at breakfast, whether for pancakes, omelettes, French toast, or waffles, threw me into utter confusion. Writing books and giving lectures seemed like easy hills to climb compared to the mountainous complexities of daily living. No wonder that I soon gave up on the idea that some of us are handicapped and others not. My handicaps were so blatantly visible in the face of what normal life is all about that I felt deeply grateful for every sign of sympathy, every smile of understanding, and, most of all, every helping hand. Maybe it was around these very down-to-earth kitchen type of things that I first started to experience the possibility of real friendship with handicapped people and their assistants. My own handicap became the way to it.

But this was obviously only the outer side of a much deeper struggle. As I entered more fully into the Daybreak community and tried to develop new and lasting relationships, I was faced with all the stresses of intimacy. My need for friendship and a deep sense of belonging had brought me to L'Arche. But the handicapped people who form the core of the community are often most wounded in places of intimacy. They easily feel rejected, disliked, put aside, or ignored and are very sensitive toward those who offer friendship, care, support, and affection. The questions are always there: Is it real? Is it lasting? Can I trust it? It is no wonder that in such a context my own anguish concerning intimate relationships was brought into the open.

I vividly remember how one of the handicapped men did not want to say "hello" to me after I had been absent for two weeks. While I felt a need to be welcomed back, he wasn't sure if I really was willing to become part of his life. And so our dark fears were rubbing up against each other and triggered off deep anguish in both of us. As he kept saying, "I don't care that you are back, I don't need your gift. I have enough things already, don't bother me. I am busy . . . ," my own deep fear of not being loved was brought to the surface, and to my own embarrassment I found myself crying uncontrollably, like a little child who feels rejected.

It was the affective wounds of the handicapped people in my own home that opened the door to my own wounded affectivity.

Very soon I was asking myself, "Do I really care for these people? Am I really willing to make them the center of my life? What do I really mean when I say to them, 'I love you'? How faithful am I really? Am I capable of a lasting relationship? Or . . . is my attention for these broken people little more than my way of feeling better about myself?" Very few stones remain unturned. Care, compassion, love for neighbor, promise, commitment, and faithfulness . . . I turned and turned these concepts in my mind and heart, and sometimes it felt as though the spiritual house I had built up over the years was now proving to be made of cardboard and ready to go up in flames. The handicapped men and women and their assistants forced me to look at myself in ways that were very humbling. Often I doubted whether there was any solid ground under my feet. I am still in the midst of this struggle, and I feel quite poor in the face of it. It is hard to discover that I am very awkward in the ordinary tasks of life. But it is much more painful for me to be brought to the realization that I am very weak and fragile precisely where I had thought I had the most to give.

But even this struggle proved not the most excruciating. Where I really was brought to my knees was at a place beyond questions about housekeeping skills, even beyond the questions about true commitment. The most radical challenge came out of the question, "Is Jesus truly enough for you, or do you keep looking for others to give you your sense of worth?" If anyone had asked me in the past, "Who is the center of your life?" I would have answered without much hesitation, "Jesus, who called me to follow him." But now I do not dare say that so easily. The struggle to become a full member of a community of faith has proved to be a struggle to let go of many idols along the way and to choose again and again to follow Jesus and him alone. Choosing life in community and choosing Jesus are increasingly appearing to me as two aspects of the same choice. And here my deepest handicap appeared.

When I came to Daybreak, I didn't come alone. Nathan, with whom I had developed a deep and nurturing friendship in Trosly, came with me. I came to Daybreak to become its pastor. He came to live as a part-time assistant while studying theology in Toronto.

As I approached the new life in community, I came to think about my friendship with Nathan as the safe place in the midst of all the transitions and changes. I said to myself, "Well, whatever happens, at least I have a friend to rely on, to go to for support, to be consoled by in hard moments." Somehow I made Nathan the center of my emotional stability and related to the life in community as something I would be able to cope with. In this way my dependence on Nathan prevented me from making the community the true center of my life. Unconsciously, I said to myself, "I already have a home. I do not really need another one." As I entered community life more deeply, however, I became gradually aware that the call to follow Jesus unreservedly required me to look for God's guidance more in the common life with handicapped people than in a unique and nurturing friendship.

This discovery created such an excruciating inner pain that it brought me to the edge of despair. I had to change my ways of coming to a sense of being accepted so radically that it seemed as if I needed to have another personality to make this come true. When I had said "yes" to the call of Daybreak to join the community as their priest, I hadn't realized how many painful "nos" were included in that "yes": "no" to choosing the people you want to live with, "no" to spending quality time with people you feel very close to, "no" to a self-defined form of solitude, "no" to centering my life in the beautiful and supportive friendship with Nathan. My many years of the independent and individualized life of a university professor had certainly not prepared me for this side of following Jesus. It led me to the second loneliness, a loneliness with Jesus in community. I discovered that this second loneliness was much, much harder to live than the loneliness resulting from physical or emotional isolation—because it is a loneliness not to be removed as a stumbling block to full human maturity, but to be embraced as the way to follow Jesus to the end.

At the end of my trip to Canada, the United States, and England, about which I wrote in this journal, I met a young man who told me about his own spiritual journey in a way that helped me to think about this second loneliness. He said, "First, I was traveling on a highway with many other people. I felt lonely in my car, but at least I was not alone. Then Jesus told me to take an exit and follow a winding country road which was pleasant and beautiful. People who passed by greeted me, smiled, and waved to me; I felt loved. But then, quite unexpectedly, Jesus asked me to take a dirt road, leave the car, and walk with him. As we were walking we did not see anyone anymore; although I knew that I was walking with Jesus, I felt very lonely and often in despair. I was tired and felt forgotten by my friends. Now it looked as if I was getting more lonely as I was getting closer to Jesus. And nobody seemed to understand."

My life at Daybreak became increasingly an invitation to enter into this second loneliness. It is such a painful experience that I hesitate to write about it. It is a loneliness of which I know no special friend can free me, even though I keep clinging desperately to such a friend. It is a loneliness that asks of me to throw myself completely into the arms of a God whose presence can no longer be felt and to risk every part of my being to what seems like nothingness. It is the loneliness of Jesus, who cries out, "My God, my God, why have you forsaken me?"

In her novel *Henry and Cato,* Iris Murdoch writes:

It's the greatest pain and the greatest paradox of all that personal love has to break at some point, the ego has to break, something absolutely natural and seemingly good, seemingly perhaps the only good, has to be given up. After that there's darkness and silence and space. And God is there. Remember St. John of the Cross. Where the images end you fall into the abyss, but it is the abyss of faith. When you have nothing left you have nothing left but hope.*

The last thing I ever expected from going to the Daybreak community was this truly abysmal experience of being ripped apart from the inside out. I expected to live with and care for mentally handicapped people, supported by a deep friendship and

* *Henry and Cato* by Iris Murdoch, Triad Grafton Books, London, 1987, p. 348.

surrounded by a beautiful network of Christian love. I was not prepared to have to deal with a second loneliness.

But . . . hesitantly and even reluctantly, I am coming to see the mystery that the community of Daybreak was given to me precisely to offer me a "safe" context in which to enter into the second loneliness with Jesus. There is nothing charming or romantic about it. It is dark agony. It is following Jesus to a completely unknown place. It is being emptied out on the cross and having to wait for new life in naked faith.

But the same cross that calls for dying from what seems so good and beautiful is also the place where a new spiritual community is being born. The death of Jesus was the dying of the grain destined to bear much fruit. My life will never be fruitful if I am not willing to go that same painful but hopeful route.

I express this with fear and trembling because I am just starting to see the light of a new day and I still do not know if I will have the courage to walk the long road ahead of me. But by writing this down I am able to look directly at my own words and that in itself is a step forward.

On July 21, 1987, I celebrated the thirtieth anniversary of my ordination to the priesthood. Considering all that I had experienced during the first year at Daybreak, I didn't feel like having a party. Instead, I asked a few of the permanent members of the community to pray with me, reflect with me on my vocation, and offer me some critical guidance. It was a very painful experience. I had to face all my handicaps directly, share them with my friends and reach out to God and the community for help. But it was also a very life-giving experience. Seeing my handicaps so clearly, those surrounding me offered all their support, guidance, and love. This helped me make them not just stumbling blocks, but gateways to solidarity with those who cannot hide their handicaps and who form the core of our community.

During this anniversary celebration, I made three promises for the years to come and asked the community to help me to be faithful to them. I want to conclude this journal by writing down these promises, to give a first articulation of the way I have begun to see the road ahead of me.

First of all, I promised to pray more. If, indeed, Jesus is the center of my life, I have to give him much time and attention. I especially want to pray the prayer of adoration in which I focus on his love, his compassion, and his mercy and not on my needs, my problems, and my desires. Much of my prayer in the past has been very introspective. The time has come to look up to him who comes to me and says, "You did not choose me, I chose you" (John 15:16). I want my life to be based on the reality of Jesus, and not on the unreality of my own fantasies, self-complaints, daydreams, and sand castles. I know that by moving from self-centered reflections to simple adoration I will come increasingly in touch with reality, the reality of God and the reality of the people of God with whom I live.

It will be very hard to be faithful to this promise. There are countless pressures to do more important things than pray. But I know that only through long and persistent prayer will I be able to follow the one who asks me to walk the lonely road with him.

Second, I promised to do everything possible to come to know my own community better. Many of the handicapped people and their assistants have remained strangers for me during this first year. The many invitations to do things outside of the community and my tendency to look for support in one or two friendships have prevented me from making the whole of the community my true home. Having meals in the different houses, "wasting time" with my own people, talking, playing, and praying with them, and allowing them to really know me, that requires a special discipline. It asks for a new way of scheduling my hours, for more "nos" to outside requests and for the strong conviction that those with whom I live are my true neighbors.

Thus I will come to know Jesus not only in the solitude of prayer, but also in the community of love. Thus the same Lord who reveals himself in the most intimate place of my heart will also reveal himself in the fellowship of the weak. It will not be easy to be faithful in this, since the temptation to search for consolation and comfort in the intimacy of a unique friendship is so great, especially during periods of depression and spiritual fatigue. My response to stress so far has been to talk it out with a spiritual director, a counselor, or a friend. It has always been in the one-to-one relationship that I have sought healing. But now I feel a strong invitation to let the community be my primary spiritual resource and to trust that there I will find the spirit of God, the true consoler I have always been looking for.

Finally, I promised to keep writing. In the generally over-scheduled life of a community such as Daybreak, it is very hard to find the quiet hours necessary to write. During the past year, writing has seemed practically impossible. And still the call to come to Daybreak included the call to keep writing. Without writing I am not truly faithful to the ministry of the word that has been given to me. It is through writing that my hidden life with God and the handicapped people can become a gift to the Church and the world. Keynote addresses, commencement speeches, and even retreats no longer seem part of my primary task. But writing still is. Many people whose judgment I trust have assured me of this. So it is up to me to discipline myself and withdraw from the urgencies and emergencies of every day and write words that emerge from my prayer and my life with the handicapped people and their assistants. Even though following Jesus might well become a more and more hidden journey for me, I do not think it should ever become a private journey. "Laying down your life for your friend" is what Jesus asks of me. For me that includes communicating as honestly as possible the pains and the joys, the darkness and the light, the fatigue and the vitality, the despair and the hope of going with Jesus to places where I would rather not go. By giving words to these intimate experiences I can make my own life available to others and thus become a witness to the word of life whom "I have heard, seen with my own eyes, watched and touched with my own hands" (1 John 1:1).

I am glad to be at Daybreak surrounded by people who want to keep me faithful to my promises. It is good to be here, even though it is hard. I feel that I have been called to be here, that I have been sent here, that I belong here. But after a year I have come to realize that I have just started on a long and arduous journey in which there will be not only many daybreaks, but also many nights. When Abraham followed God's call, he had no idea how much would be asked of him. His faith would be tested every step of the way. This is true for everyone God calls with a "jealous" love. Even though I keep daydreaming about an easy and conflict-free tomorrow, I know that *my* faith too will be tested. God's love is indeed "a harsh and dreadful thing" (Dorothy Day) but worth giving one's whole life for.

This brings me to the end of this journal. I have tried to describe carefully the road that led me to Daybreak, to express honestly my first experiences here, and to lay out frankly the promises I have made for the future. It is becoming increasingly clear to me that Jesus led me to where I never wanted to go, sustained me when I felt lost in the darkness of the night, and will guide me toward the day no longer followed by night. As I travel with Jesus, he continues to remind me that God's heart is, indeed, infinitely greater than my own.

About the Author

Henri J. M. Nouwen was born in the Netherlands, where he was ordained to the priesthood. He has taught at the University of Notre Dame, Yale Divinity School, and Harvard Divinity School. His works include *Creative Ministry, The Wounded Healer, Reaching Out,* and *Lifesigns.* In 1986 he became the priest for Daybreak, L'Arche community in Toronto, Canada.

THE TREASURY OF HENRI J. M. NOUWEN

AVAILABLE AT YOUR LOCAL BOOKSTORE OR YOU MAY USE THIS COUPON TO ORDER DIRECT.

ISBN	TITLE AND AUTHOR	PRICE	QTY.	TOTAL
17446-2	**The Genesee Diary** by Henri J. M. Nouwen *Report from a Trappist Monastery*	$8.95	x ___ =	_____
00918-6	**Aging** by Henri J. M. Nouwen and Walter J. Gaffney *The Fulfillment of Life*	$9.95	x ___ =	_____
18957-5	**Compassion** by Henri J. M. Nouwen, Donald P. McNeil, and Douglas A. Morrison *A Reflection on the Christian Life*	$9.95	x ___ =	_____
12616-6	**Creative Ministry** by Henri J. M. Nouwen *A Spiritual Guide for Christians*	$9.95	x ___ =	_____
23628-X	**Lifesigns** by Henri J. M. Nouwen *Intimacy, Fecundity, and Ecstasy* *in Christian Perspective*	$8.95	x ___ =	_____
23682-4	**Reaching Out** by Henri J. M. Nouwen *The Three Movements of the* *Spiritual Life*	$9.95	x ___ =	_____
41607-5	**The Road to Daybreak** by Henri J. M. Nouwen *A Spiritual Journey*	$11.00	x ___ =	_____
14803-8	**The Wounded Healer** by Henri J. M. Nouwen *"Nouwen at his best"*	$7.95	x ___ =	_____

SHIPPING AND HANDLING:
Parcel Post . . . . (add $2.50 per order; allow 4–6 weeks for delivery) _____
UPS . . . . (add $4.50 per order; allow 2–3 weeks for delivery) _____
TOTAL: _____

Please send me the titles I have indicated above. I am enclosing $ _____.
Send check or money order (no CODs or cash, please) payable to Doubleday
Consumer Services. Prices and availability are subject to change without notice.

Name:_____

Address:_____ Apt. #:_____

City:_____ State:_____ Zip:_____

Send completed coupon and payment to:
Doubleday Consumer Services, Dept. IM11
2451 South Wolf Road
Des Plaines, IL 60018

IMAGE

IM11 - 11/95